SOUTH

PEOPLE
AND
PLACES

Written and Compiled
by
past and present members of
C.L.A.S.S.

FIDUCIA PRESS

2004

SOUTHVILLE
PEOPLE
AND
PLACES

Written and compiled
by
past and present members of
C.L.A.S.S.
(Continued Learning for Adults at South Street)

Editing and Book Design
by
Roy Gallop and Ken Griffiths

Cover photograph: Dean Lane looking towards North Street. The terrace on the left is still there. On the right is St. Paul's Church School, built in 1872 and demolished in 1959. The photograph is undated but there are indications that it was taken before the turn of the 20th century.

Title page: The entrance to Gaol ferry, a 1913 drawing by S J Loxton. The archway under Coronation Road led up into Southville Road and Acramans Road. Access to Coronation Road by path and steps is still there below the Gaol Ferry Bridge.

Back cover: A 1910 view across the New Cut to Coronation Road, St. Pauls Church and the Gaol Ferry by S J Loxton. Mr Edwin Cox of Hanham, who, as a child lived in Boot Lane, Bedminster, recently recalled that his father Frederick, as a young man, effected a rescue of a ferryman who fell from his craft.

Published by FIDUCIA Press, 10 Fairfield Road, Southville, Bristol, BS3 1LG. Copyright C.L.A.S.S. All rights reserved: No part of this book may be reproduced, or transmitted in any other form or by means electronic or mechanical, including photocopying, recording or by any information storage retrieval system, without the written permission of the publishers.

© FIDUCIA PRESS   ISBN 0 946217 16 5
Printed in Great Britain by Doveton Press Ltd., of Bristol

CONTENTS

Preface	4
Introduction	5
Industry and Commerce	8
Southville Roads	15
Southville Churches	27
Women	30
Landowners	33
Schools	39
Medical Matters	50
Police, Law and Order	55
Southville Voices	61
Appendix	63
Sources and Acknowledgements	64

A 1950s photograph of East Street (Nelson Parade) with Zion Chapel at the commencement of Coronation Road. At top left is the chimney of the tannery in Stillhouse Lane. Top centre, also in Stillhouse Lane is Bristol Technical School. (Engineering Dept.) Most of these buildings were demolished for the doubling of Bedminster Bridge.

This project was researched and written by Georgia Lewis and her friends and is dedicated to her memory.

PREFACE

For this history, our borders basically follow that of the 1845 Tythe Map of Southville. That is, the entire length of Coronation Road from old Zion Church to the Toll House at Ashton Gate. Here Coronation Road joins with the thoroughfare of North Street. A small area of this route links briefly with Ashton, but in Southville history this area was owned and worked by Southville people.

We follow North Street on the left until it meets with Dean Lane. All roads, lanes and alleys, however crooked, leading from North Street are important tracks to Southville. We include the Star Inn. This hostelry was not only owned and operated by Southville people; in earlier days it served as a Court of Justice for the area. Booth Road, the shortest street in the area, now home of the Salvation Army, is a historical part of Southville, backing as it does on to Dame Emily Park, once the Dean Lane coal pit. Roads leading from Dean Lane on the right towards East Street are vital places in Southville's past. Some roads have now gone; others remain in part; some have been drastically altered. A few remain, such as Dean Street, Lombard Street and Dean Crescent.

The main Bedminster Causeway has been well documented historically and appears in our volume only as it affected Southville people. For example, the Bedminster Police Station was the only law enforcement place for Southville people; the Public Library was the main outlet for reading materials and many Bedminster meeting halls, churches, public houses and places of entertainment were attended by residents of our area.

A direct route through Dean Lane passes by the sites of the old mine and the the coal rail line. Dean Lane was once the home of the St. Paul's schools and the Mission House of St. Paul's. Some of Southville's oldest houses were along this route together with some of Southville's earliest shops and businesses. Much has disappeared and in this history we will attempt to re-create the past.

Dean Lane connects with Coronation Road, but if the visitor turns before this up Stackpool Road you enter the place where substantial houses of the wealthy stood. History buffs now pass through the most historic part of Southville, the ancient Perry Hill district. Southville Junior School is on the site of the haunted Merrywood Hall. From here the route may be taken to the right down one of the very steep roads back to Coronation Road, or to the left by way of Greville Road back to North Street and the Hen and Chicken. Yet another way would be along Raleigh Road, past the Wills Ashton buildings and once again to North Street.

The map will help the visitor to follow the area, but only the following pages will reveal the wealth of history to be discovered in Southville.

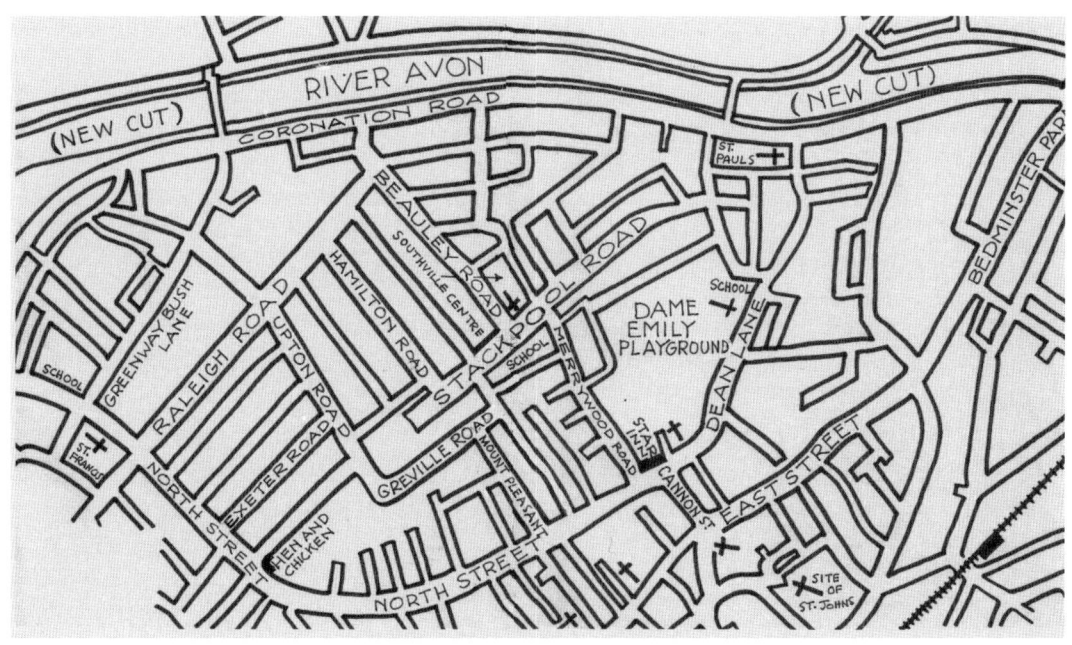

SKETCH MAP OF SOUTHVILLE

INTRODUCTION

Beneath the quiet respectability of Southville, historical records reveal intrigue, feuds, cruelty and violence, interlayered with benevolence, solicitude and good humour.

The district was first known as Great Perry Hill, due to the large pear orchards there, a name which remains in the small terrace of Upper Perry Hill and until the 1890s in several terraces on North Street. This is also the site, identified by Ashmead's Map of 1826/8 of the mock fort, built for the visit of Queen Elizabeth I in 1574. The height of the site, now known as the top of Osborne Road, was equivalent to that of Brandon Hill, facing it from the other side of the Avon. To ensure that the firework display put on by the City delighted the Queen the fort would have been well built. A large contingent of workmen and officials came to this place, south of the river to guarantee a splendid show. No one wished to risk losing his head! Perhaps it was one of these people who dropped the shilling, found almost four centuries later by Mr. Laurie Phillips of Islington Road.

St Katherine's Hospice, situated where Asda is today and which was demolished to make way for the old Wills tobacco factory, was a medieval link with Southville. The Malago flowed through the hospital's grounds which went close by where Dean Lane is today. The institution, which included a hostelry, was a gathering place for festivals, processions, stage entertainment and meetings. People from Ashton and the other side of town, after crossing the Avon, would have walked through the future 'Southville'. The monastic order attached to St Katherine's was closed by Henry VIII in 1539 but the hospital continued to exist for three more centuries.

A map made from the notes of William Wyrecester in 1480 and drawn up in 1860 in *Bristol Past and Present* by Nicolls & Taylor, names this land as 'Catherine Mead', a name remembered today as Catherine Mead Street. Ogilby's Road Map of 1698, referred to by Latimer in *Annals of the 18th Century*, states that the land was known as Bedminster Meadows. It was known as such by John Hare, who slept in these fields overnight in 1773, and vowed to build a church here one day. More than fifty years later, in 1830, he built Zion Church on this spot.

The Malago flowed through St Katherine's into Treen Mills. In 1774 Sydenham Teast, who owned the land where the first sod of the New Cut would be dug in 1804, advertised Treen Mills to be let. The advertisement read "The Mills are supplied by fresh tide water and also with a stream of fresh water". The stream, the Malago, provided early Southville people with clear water, and was used for food, medicinal purposes and also for recreation. Small craft navigated the stream for centuries.

Treen Mills was excavated in 1805 to form Bathurst Basin. St Augustine's Church, which owned the rights of this land, was compensated for the loss of the Mills by Bristol Corporation in 1809. It is not recorded how much was paid to Mr Teast. The Malago was diverted to exit into the Cut when the latter was created, but the stream literally popped up at various places along and close to Coronation Road for many years. The Malago was not tamed until the 20th century and continued to flood for many decades.

Early accounts of Bristol either ignore South Bristol or depict the future land of Southville as being uninhabited. The name Southville was not used until the early 19th century, but the Manor of Bedminster is described in the Doomsday Book (1087). Artefacts including coins, military curios, ancient remains of stone walls, old wells and brooks (now covered) are evidence that Southville land was well used, if not well populated, long before records became available.

Records of the late 17th century show Bedminster and some parts of what would be Southville to be most active. The Smyth family bought the Bedminster Manor in 1605 and the incumbent paid for the title of 'Sir' in 1613 from King James. Since this time private bands of militia carried out manoeuvers on Southville's hills, marshes and fields. Sir John Smyth and his successor took good care of their Southville lands. Smyth made a practice of touring his holdings and meeting tenants at the Star Inn in the 18th century to see if his profits were enlarged.

It is a matter of record that the Hen and Chicken on North Street, predates The Cut. Documents of 1741 prove that buildings, named as 'dwellings', stood on the future Coronation Road and Greenway Bush Lane and some of the oldest houses in Southville, 'cottages' in Dean Lane, were older than the Cut. We have noted the activities at St Katherine's and there is documentary evidence that industry was beginning in the 18th century in the future area of Coronation Road and adjacent land.

Thus from north and south, east and west, Southville, while not heavily populated, certainly had people living and working in the area. Most Coronation Road houses have huge cellars, and some bricked up arches, giving rise to legends of sanctuaries and smuggling. St John's, the Parish Church of Bedminster since 1086, had come under the whip of Henry VIII and a priest was hanged.

By order of Prince Rupert the church was pillaged and burned in September 1645 during the Civil War. The lands of the church adjoined and spilled over to Southville. Dwellings of priests and small monasteries were burned down at this time. The old name of Abbots Lane, where Merrywood Hall was later built, is believed to date from this time of suppression, so that a small monastic order might well have stood in this place.

The homogeneous group of people who owned or occupied land in early Southville were representative of a changing society. While the Smyth family and the Gore-Langtons were officially listed in 1845 as 'Lords of the Manor', the feudal manorial system was fast changing. However, in the early 1800s, the Manor Lords, bonded by marriage and other close family ties, owned two thirds of the area. They owned it side by side with the hog merchants, shopkeepers, tanners, iron manufacturers, publicans, ship owners, scavenger operators and professional people.

Most owners had powerful connections through the dominant Merchant Venturers Society, politics, esoteric trade links, religion and the bond of family. They were mostly all wealthy. This factor, empowered with influence and interdependence in trade and shipping, ensured that the New Cut would pass through or close by their property, so enhancing the value.

Like the deep tunnels which run under many Southville houses, a host of secrets remain buried. Some Southville people see and hear ghosts. It is said that ghostly sounds come from the Cut, where many were lost when it was being excavated. There are Southville residents who still remember the ghosts of Merrywood Hall (where Merrywood Junior school was built later) and perhaps not too surprisingly from Zion Chapel.

Ships, boats and various smaller types of sailing vessels plied the Cut for over 100 years. There are many stories of smuggling. In the early 19th century, and indeed the middle and latter part of it, the smuggling of certain goods by way of the Cut would have prevented hefty dock dues.

Plenty of wealthy and influential folk lived in the area. One needs but to look at the list of people who requested, in March 1828, that St Paul's Church be built in Southville and a further list of those who attended the stone-laying ceremony eighteen months later on September 12th 1829. Mayors, past and future, Sheriffs, both in office then and in future years and Merchant Venturer's officials, were side by side with rich businessmen, solicitors and policy makers. It is interesting also that such a number of representatives and agents of European countries chose to live in Southville.

Sir A B Mascrenhas, Consul for Portugal, lived at Stroud Building, Coronation Road, in 1833 and his son who also lived there, was Vice Consul. E Fedden, who lived at Merrrywood Hall was Consul for Brazil; H Visger, a powerful influence in Southville, also living in Coronation Road, was Consul for Prussia; H G Flower, Southville landowner, was Consul for France. Others, notably Acraman, Visger and Flower, were members of the Chamber of Commerce, Trade and Manufacturers. By the 1880s, the Manor Lords, ever in need of money, began to sell off their land. It was bought up by developers and builders: Kingston, Bennett, Davis, Pine, Summons and Latham. As residents became secure in jobs at Wills in East Street and Raleigh Road and with Robinsons in Bedminster, they bought their own houses. Southville grew and prospered, populated by a diversity of people whose lives and stories will be revealed in the following chapters.

INDUSTRY and COMMERCE

The early industrialists of Southville were all pillars of St Paul's Church or Zion Chapel. The Bayntons supported St Paul's and owned several large Bedminster coach businesses, making 'improved' Swiss charrettes on four wheels. Other early industrials included the Chandlers, who owned part of the Bedminster Brewery, the Drakes who owned the Bedminster Tannery, William Goulstone part-owner of the North Street coal pit, the Goughs of the Bedminster Mill family and Charles Hill of the renowned shipyard; all endorsed St Paul's Church. Hill's Shipyard continued to employ Southville workers until well after we end our story.

Charles Hill began work in 1810 in the management of Hillhouse dockyards. In 1827 he married Mary Arthur, a relative by marriage to the Hillhouses. The Hillhouse Dockyard became Charles Hill & Sons. Charles Hill was closely associated with St Paul's and in 1830 was a churchwarden. In 1842 he was the first elected peoples warden of St Pauls. He died in 1867 leaving two sons who took over the running of the Albion Dockyard.

The industrialists who attended Zion Church were John Hare and his family (who owned the Oil Cloth Factory at Temple Gate) and also the Wills Brothers. E S & A Robinson's Printing Works in Bedminster was a large employer of Southville people. Robinsons had first had a factory at Redcliffe but in 1886 opened the Bedminster Works and those Southville people not working at Wills rushed to get jobs at Robinsons. Mr Frank Pring's father, William, was one of the earliest to get a job and the family swiftly moved into Kingston Road, even as it was being built.

Robinsons had from early times been interested in Southville. One of the family, E Robinson, had bought land on the Dean Lane curve in 1850 from J H G Smyth. This land went up from Dean Lane (where St Paul's Mission house was later built) almost as far as Stackpool Road and back almost to Merrywood Lane. The Robinson Family had thought of creating a factory there. The property was close to the Bedminster Tannery and to the Dean Lane mine, so that all facilities of transport and workers were close at hand. The residents of Acraman and Alpha Roads and of the Dean Lane cottages at the back of this property were not pleased by the proposal and E S Robinson, very sensitive to public feeling, abandoned the plan. He sold the property through Smyth to William Panes Kingston in 1881. Robinson was very active in politics, serving on the Council and held many elected positions (eg Guardian for Bristol

South). The Robinson family lived on a large estate at Sneyd Park. E S Robinson died in August 1886, the year before his Bedminster factory opened. But he saw most of it built and it was always called E S & A Robinson. Robinson donated money to all the area's churches and his workers 'shared' services with Wills employees - there were not enough churches built at the time. The two large businesses also shared social functions and pooled resources, especially at the time they were both recovering from the moving of their factories to Bedminster. The powerful of Southville attended Robinson's huge funeral. A bust of him is in the Colston Hall.

Henry Overton Wills, born on 2nd March, 1761 in Salisbury, Wiltshire, was the first in the family to enter the tobacco business. He is registered in the Bristol Trade Directory in 1786 as a partner in the tobacco business of Wills, Watkins & Co, In the late 18th Century treating tobacco leaf was normally done by women and girls, who even in those days were two thirds of the workforce and paid on on their output. Working in confined areas in the early years with the fumes and speed of work, many of the girls suffered lung infections in their late teens and did not recover. After the retirement of Watkins in 1789 the firm was renamed H O Wills & Co and the following year Henry Overton Wills married Anne Day, the daughter of a linen draper in the city. Henry and Ann lived in Redcliffe Street and by 1807 they had five children. Anne, born November 1792; William Day, born June 1797; Mary, born January 1799; Henry Overton II, born July 1800 and Frederick, born June 1804.

In 1808, a pressing need for larger working premises arose in Redcliffe Street and H O Wills withdrew £420 from the business to buy a house on Redcliffe Hill. It was thought to be one of a small terrace of Georgian houses directly opposite St Mary Redcliffe Church, which gave one of the finest outlooks in Bristol. The Revd. William Day was brother-in-law of H O Wills. In June 1818 the marriage took place of Anne Wills, oldest daughter of Henry and Anne, to William Day Junior, who were first cousins. On his marriage, William Day was given a sixth share in the partnership and a capital sum of £500. Their married life was very short. Anne died after four years, at the age of thirty. Henry Overton Wills, her father, fell ill and died on 2nd December 1826. His will requested that his son, H O Wills II, be his successor in a business he had headed for forty years and provided a very large amount of capital for a great part of that time. Anne's husband, William Day, died two years later in 1828, when he was thirty-eight. As there were no surviving children, William's estate (except the capital credited to his partnership) was divided between various members of his family.

The two brothers W D & H O Wills headed the business at the ages of thirty-four and thirty, respectively. Henry Overton Wills who was married twice and had eighteen children was later to figure as H O Wills III. He played an important part in the 19th and 20th Centuries with the building of two new factories. Production was improved thirty years after the cutting machine was introduced and the tobacco was also packed by machine. Wills gave many famous names to their tobacco, which became known world wide.

In 1847 when the railways were expanding in every direction, brand names were given to two of the tobaccos - Best Bird's Eye and Bishop Blaze - assuring smokers of the quality at all times. It was also sold to retailers without technical knowledge. (At one time trade was only given to tobacco specialists.) In 1883, Henry Wills obtained the British patent of the American Bonsack cigarette machine with an output of two hundred a minute. This enabled the cost of production to be slashed. In 1886, W D & H O Wills opened the No 1 Factory in East Street, Bedminster. It was a large modern building and the first to be installed with electric light. This brought work and trade to the area and the people of Southville welcomed the change. 1878 saw the first use of 'stiffeners' in the paper packets they carried advertisements for the Company's products, which was later changed to the cigarette card. In 1888 'Wild Woodbines' were produced at five for a penny and demand was so great that machines were fixed to walls so that the cigarettes could be purchased if shops were shut. 'Cinderella', another brand on the market at the same time, sold at the same price.

The first cigar advertised, named 'Rajah', appeared in 1897 and 'Golden Virgina' held a leading position as the handrolling tobacco brand. Castella 'Panatellas' remained the best selling cigars and were always associated with a pint of beer. H O Wills was expanding his trade and looking for another suitable place for his second factory in the area.

Wills former factory and offices in East Street, Bedminster, opened in 1886 and vacated in 1975.

In 1901 Wills amalgamated with twelve other manufacturers to fight off American competition. The firm became W D & H O Wills' branch of the I T Company, known as the Imperial Tobacco Company (of Great Britain and Ireland). The offices were in the front of the Bedminster building. Wills took over a building in Raleigh Road, already a busy thoroughfare in Southville, and opened it as Factory No 4 - a bonded factory. It was transferred to the British American Tobacco Company from 1902 until 1919.

In 1901 Wills bought ten acres of ground in Ashton, which took in the railed-off playing fields at North Street and Raleigh Road. This was the old cricket ground where W G Grace had played. Constructed of the best materials the walls in places were 21" and 36" in width, giving added strength. The architecture was of the finest with designed craftwork making it a unique building in the area. Franklyn Davy, a subsidiary, occupied the front part of the building in North Street. They produced a superfine tobacco named 'Honeydew'. They also made two brands of cigarettes, one named 'Loadstone' and a special brand called 'Royals', which was double the length of the average cigarette. Wills also manufactured 'Five Star Bar' for them. It was the ambition of many school leavers to work for the firm. Lots were disappointed as the waiting list was long. For many years it was run on a family basis and privilege was given to those who already had someone working there to speak for them.

Most of the employees started in the stripping room and the new ones could always be spotted with plasters on their fingers, sore from stripping the leaf and the speed at which they worked to reach their quota. Seventy pound was the basic weight for a day's work and any more was a bonus on the week's wages. Hand-picked girls, with long fingers, were generally chosen for the cigar factory, where some brands were individually rolled by hand. Wills introduced another popular cigarette, the 'Star'. These were sold at 4d. for ten which was the price which suited the average person.

Houses at the top end of Raleigh Road were owned by The Imperial Tobacco Company. Known as Raleigh Cottages they ran in a block of three. Two belonged to the staff of Wills and the third was owned by Franklyn Davy. A large warehouse stored the cardboard boxes, silver paper and cigarette cards. Four more houses were occupied by security staff. Further along, No 7, was the Transport Department and garages on the end opened into Upton Road. No 8, the tin case factory, owned by Ashton Containers since 1920, was in Upton Road towards Greenway Bush

Cigarette making in the Wills factory in Bedminster in 1910.

Lane, on the right hand side. The tins, made by hand, were used for Virginian snuff, which was produced there from the crushed leaf stems and loose tobacco dust. In 1932 competition became keen and Wills brought out a cigarette named 'Four Aces' with a free gift scheme catalogue of practical gifts, to ward off competition.

Whatever obstacles they may have hit, W D & H O Wills always gave the best they could to their workers. Everything in the way of medical care was provided 'free of charge' for their employees. A bonus was paid to Wills workers around the 8th March and shops seemed to know this because folk always said the prices rose around that time. The Wills employees were strongly encouraged to be church-goers and to engage in community activities. They needed to be stalwart to survive working at Wills. After a long day's work the employees felt duty bound to participate in sports. Women were particularly urged to excel in home-making skills and sang in choirs, in order to advance their salaries. Early Wills 'in-house' magazines, which can be found in the Central Library, record an astonishing number of deaths of young women employees. Whilst various wasting diseases (consumption) caused early deaths everywhere, the tobacco dust fumes appeared to add to their ill-health.

The formation of the BBC in 1922 benefited Southville business firms, shops, etc. Shops opened up in the area to serve the new wireless enthusiasts. Two types of wireless were available - a valve and battery set in a smart cabinet, which proved too expensive for most, or alternatively, a simple crystal set which did not require a battery. An outside aerial conducted the signal which was so weak it could only be heard through headphones. It was tuned by touching the crystal with a springy wire or a 'cat's whisker' as it was called. Reception was easily lost through the slightest noise, even a sneeze.

Some Southville people may recall the early programmes of the BBC. There was no news before 7pm (for fear that newspaper sales would fall) and sporting events did not include the results. On Sundays, comedy, light music and popular discussions were banned. Despite this the wireless was popular in our area, especially children's programmes. Just before 6 o'clock family arguments were settled on who should have the headsets because 'Children's Hour' was broadcast at 6pm every evening, Monday to Saturday, with the BBC's own cast of 'Uncles' and 'Aunties'. A new relay station was opened every month throughout 1924. 'The Radio Times' was first published on 28th September 1923. In the General Election of 1924 the leaders of each political party made its first broadcast - Stanley Baldwin (Conservative), who won the Election, Herbert Asquith (Liberal) and Ramsey Macdonald (Labour).

The wireless reception was maintained by re-charging the batteries. Made of glass, they were large and heavy and care was needed when they were returned to be re-charged. Another battery would be exchanged and the wireless was not left dormant. Hassells, builders who owned the one storey shop in Stackpool Road near the turning into Greville Street, supplied this service. Hills, the Magneto works in Morley Road, started in the mid-20s by producing wireless parts. Small corner shops benefited from changing batteries and selling parts to DIY enthusiasts. By the late 20s the wireless created a boom for small Southville businesses.

A 1930s photograph of number 244 North Street.

E N Miles - The Drapers

"From the London Inn three miles to the Town Hall" was an expression locals associated with the popular store E N Miles & Co, Drapers Ltd.

Egbert Nathaniel Miles left the family home in North Pembrokeshire to join his uncle, John Picton, who owned a shop on Redcliffe Hill. He, E N Miles, opened the first of the three shops in Cannon Street in 1896. Mr Miles, a tall handsome man, loved people and had an uncanny memory for names and faces as he greeted everyone with a joke or soothing enquiry while walking down Merrywood Road to his business. A favourite saying of his was "The person you are serving is the most important person in your life." His belief in hard work combined with a sense of fun appealed to the people of Southville who flocked to the Cannon Street Stores. Today he might be called a workaholic, for he worked long hours and loved it.

Extra female assistants were employed as business prospered, and a delivery service was started, giving two positions to errand boys. They rode the traditional carrier bikes with basket and advertised the shop's name on a metal strip beneath the bar. The three shops carried a wide range of goods. Bargains placed in the porchway attracted passers-by and window displays advertised the stock each shop carried. The interiors were long and narrow with wood flooring, each

Cannon Street, looking towards North Street. E N Miles shops sandwiched between the London Inn and the old Town Hall.

identical. On each side of the shop door a dark oak counter was raised on a wooden platform with a rim which made an ideal foot rest. Two or three high chairs were placed at each counter, which ended where a walk-through gave access to the three shops. An overhead rail ran the length of the counter in the household shop carrying remnants and bargains to catch the customer's eye while waiting to be served. The stores acted as social centres for shoppers and friends. "I'll just sit down for five minutes" was a familiar phrase, and many confidences and scandals were analysed in comfortable settings. The assistants kept the same counter, gaining experience with stock, which became beneficial when serving.

Most of the unwrapped stock was kept dust free in wall cabinets with drawers, flush sliding glass doors, protected trays and hard case containers and boxes were also kept on shelves within easy reach of the assistants. These would be brought to the counter when the garments could be sorted for choice and opened out before a purchase was made. Although the tills were available, a receipt book with the shop heading was always used, and when more than one item was purchased the total was checked and signed by another assistant before being paid in at

Mr E N Miles

A 1920s photograph of the sweet and tobacconist shop, J Stacey, at the Cannon Street end of North Street.

the cash desk at the far end of the middle shop. Near the cash desk a haberdashery cabinet displayed trays of lingerie and a large selection of corsetry was stocked. A popular line was their famous 'Tea Rose' corset at 47 shillings a dozen - what a picture of days long gone this conjures up.

The first shop next to the London Inn stocked household merchandise. The bedding was at the far end of the shop with rolls of curtain material. Ready-made curtains were also displayed together with heavy table cloths. A wide range of garments for adults, underwear, nightwear, daywear, hosiery, etc, was kept in the front section of the middle shop.

The third shop catered for babies and older children, and a cabinet displayed merchandise in this line. Haberdashery was also stocked in this shop. Club cards were introduced which allowed customers to save a regular amount each week from January to mid-October. When the club closed, the total was added and 1s 8d in the pound bonus given. Purchases with the card were made from 1st November until Christmas. During this time, customers packed the shop and employers also helped with the serving.

The staff suffered tired legs and aching feet, as customers were allowed to have all their items on the one visit which meant assistants fetching requirements from other departments. Sighs of relief and satisfaction must have been felt on Christmas Eve after having served the numerous customers who passed through the doors of E N Miles & Company.

SOUTHVILLE ROADS

The oldest part of Southville borders the Coronation Road area. Before the digging of the Cut commenced, fields stretched right across to the floating harbour. North Street was in existence long before 1801, although it was only known by this name from that date. Quite a few people lived in Southville at this time, either in small cottages, such as Dean Cottage, dotted around the area, or in large mansions. Gardeners were the main occupiers, although business and professional people and also publicans lived there. The New Cut was constructed between 1804-1809, during which time the first Bedminster Bridge was built in 1807. Across from the Cut the New Gaol was taking shape, the foundation stone laid in 1816 and the building completed by 1820.

One of the main thoroughfares of today, Coronation Road was opened in 1822. It was named to commemorate the Coronation of King George IV. Men who worked on the road were treated to a feast to celebrate. Trafalgar Place appears at this time, too. In 1825 this was intersected by Charlotte Street, probably named at the same time as Coronation Road, after the Princess Charlotte Augusta (1796-1817), daughter of George IV. Building along Coronation Road began to increase and by 1828 Alpha Cottages, Wellington Terrace and Richmond Place were in existence. Queen Street and King Street were also built at this time. Wellington Terrace obviously named after the Duke and King and Queen Street to commemorate their Majesties. Greenway Place built in 1829 in Dean Lane could have been named after a Mr Greenway who was still living there in 1841. Dean Lane, built in 1839, was much narrower than we know it today.

This photograph shows the rebuilt church of St. Paul's Southville. The original was destroyed in the blitz on Bristol during World War 2.

In North Street there used to be Carlton Place, built in 1830. A Counting House stood there, No 1 Carlton Place, built by the well-known publisher, Joseph Cottle. Farley's Square appears in 1831, believed to have been situated between Regent Road and Coronation Road. Ashton Place appears in 1850, Ashton Terrace on Coronation Road was already in existence prior to 1844, as was Greenway Bush Lane. Building was gradually extending along Coronation Road. Russell Terrace and Nelson Terrace were built in 1852. Clarence Place, Southville Place and Florence Place were there in 1858, the latter consisting of only three buildings. Later on, in 1870, No 1 was occupied by a school owned by Mr J J Newton; in No 2 lived Mr W G Kinnock an accountant and in No 3 was Mr Hull a grocer. Florence Place was demolished in 1986. The houses behind the old police station were also built in 1858.

In the year 1861 at No 2 Laura Villas, Alpha Road, lived Captain Browne and his family. He was Captain of the 'Lord Petre' a barque. At the same time living in Southville Place was Captain R Keats of the ship 'Bristolian'. In 1867 Mrs. Elizabeth Board was living in Trafalgar Place. She was the widow of James Board and mother of Mr. Thomas Board of the Bristol Distillery. During the 1870s many new streets and roads were laid in the Southville area. In 1870 Acramans Road, which extends from Dean Lane to Southville Road, contained in all fifteen residences. The buildings were mainly privately owned villas, with their own names. The road itself was named after the Acraman family, who were prominent in civic and commercial life in the first half of the 19th century.

Situated behind St Paul's church in Southville Road was the entrance to the Gaol Ferry and nearby was Newton Cottage. On the opposite side of the road stood Mona Lodge, now occupied by Thomas Davis, Funeral Directors and renamed Southville Lodge. The Rev. T Ward lived at the Vicarage, now the Chapel of Rest. Next to this was Eastfield House. Further along Coronation Road we find Coronation Villas, which consisted of four houses built between Ashton Terrace and Lower Ashton Terrace. Next to the Avon Packet Tavern public house were two houses named Greenbank Villas. Greenbank Road intersected here, then a house, Victoria Cottage, Clift Cottage and lastly the Ashton turnpike. Bull Lane which ran from North Street up to Merrywood Hall was renamed Merrywood Lane. In 1871 Essex Street was being constructed and Bethesda Chapel built at this time. The street was completed by 1873.

In Regent Street there was Nelson gardens, also Fletchers Court, Murch's Buildings in Queen Street and in King Street there were Railway Cottages and Waterloo Square. A busy thoroughfare today, Catherine Mead Street was built in 1874 and contained Lombard Terrace. Lombard Street had been built previously in 1872. About this time trees were planted along the side of the New Cut in Coronation Road. During the late 1870s and for the next twenty years or more Southville became a larger and more thriving area. The building started with the opening in 1879 of Stackpool Road, then spelt 'Stackpole'. It commenced at Dean Lane and finished at the top of Merrywood Lane. Many of these streets are now replaced by multi-story flats and Asda car park.

Dean Lane

Dean Lane was an old and busy thoroughfare before Southville was officially recorded.

Business people and traders were occupying some of the villas in 1870. Robert J Crocker, Builder, lived in 'Parnicott House' and Edward Mallard, the Tax Collector, resided in 'Paradise Gardens'. Bevan & Son, Builders, formerly of North Street, Bedminster, moved to Dean Lane, near the Clarence Hotel and Paradise Gardens in 1873. The following year they moved to Merrywood Lane and were in business there until 1880. H T Bevan resided for a time at 'Larna Cottage', Southville. In 1875 shops started to open in the Lane. These included W Appleby, Baker, of North Street, Bedminster since 1840 and G Bennett, Baker, also of North Street since 1870. A third baker, J Talbot, 'business-wise', put his roots in the ground and never looked back. He had his own bakery in a separate building in the yard at the back of the shop with access to a lane which opened into Herbert Street. John W Delaney, Chemist and Druggist and Analytical Chemist and F T Woodcock, were also trading in the Lane in 1875.

Opposite Stackpool Road were three cottages, 'Camden', which was occupied by Miss Baker Eliza Maies School in 1870 and William Charles, Plasterer, in 1890. The other two were 'Isleworth' and 'Devonshire'. In 1880 a plumber, fitter and decorator had moved into 'Catherine House', 31 Dean Lane and W P Kingston, Builder occupied 'Lindthorpe House', higher up in Dean Lane. This is now the Doctors' surgery. On the corner of Stackpool Road and Dean Lane was 'The Southville Supply Stores', the property of Joshua Nunn, previously a tea dealer and grocer, 1886. Next to the stores was Russell Terrace with four houses. The last in line was 'Bermuda Lodge' on the corner of Dean Lane and Coronation Road. By 1900 more shops had opened.

No 43 Dean Lane
Clarence Hotel, now the Tap & Barrel was built in Dean Lane in 1873. The first licensee until 1876 was Elizabeth Armstrong. Subsequent Landlords were:-
        David Harris - 1877 - 1882
        Richard Matthews - 1883
        E Gunning - 1884
        W E Wookey - 1885 - 1886
J H Coombs became Landlord in 1887 and the Hotel ran as a family business for many years. Ada Maud, his wife, took charge from 1910 to 1932. Reginald, their son became Landlord in 1932. He was a respected man, recognized in his later years as a 'Stately Old Gent'. Distinguished in his plus-fours and dickie-bow tie, which was always part of his attire. The Clarence had a large room upstairs which was used for entertainment. The Hotel was also the favourite haunt of the coal miners from Dean Lane Pit opposite. It was from here they collected their money on payday, much to the delight, no doubt, of the Landlord, as the miners probably spent half of their wages there before going home.

No 47 Dean Lane

Guy Arthur Pearce obtained the property 1924/32. Frank Pope, owner of the cycle shop, made a deal with Arthur to purchase his shop for a cycle repair depot. Keeping his living quarters above the business, Arthur continued making humbugs and coconut bars in the flat. He obtained a tricycle with a box carrier on the front and sold his produce in the streets. Entry to his flat was made through the shop during opening hours. Alternatively he used the back entrance in the side lane, next to the shop. He was still living and trading from there in 1940.

It is known, but only by word of mouth, as the Deeds have not been seen in later years, that No 51 Dean Lane originally belonged to the mines. Consisting of a shop and large living quarters, the rooms over the front of the shop are normal size. The area at the back has a large loft covering the rest of the building, which could have been used for machinery. The Bristol Education Committee opened the building as a Clinic for school children in the area in 1925. It was closed in 1936 when a new Clinic was built in St Johns Lane. George Thomas Tame opened a newsagent at No 53 in 1897/98; George Thomas Henry, Civil and Military Tailor, in 1898/1901; William Seal, Carpenter, owned the business premises 1901/04; James Hollier, General Dealer, purchased the property in 1904. He became a Phonograph Dealer in 1911 and was selling gramophones and violins in 1940.

George Stenner, Haulier, owned No 59, 1899/1900; Thomas Serle, Builder, 1900/09; Stone and Pryer, Builders, purchased the building from S Thomas in 1923 and sold out to Walter Summerhayes in 1927. A Greengrocer, he also had side interests. He kept pigeons with one of his sons and the loft can still be seen in the yard at the side of the house. Members of the Bedminster South Pigeon Club, which was held at the back of the London Inn, took the pigeons in carriers to Temple Meads every friday. All ringed, they were taken on journeys and then let free to see whose pigeon was the fastest getting back to their loft. In a stable at the back of the house was the favourite white horse, 'Dolly'. She was groomed and entered in the Horse and Cart Shows at Horfield.

In 1908, Clark's Wood and Timber Merchants of Coronation Road since 1820, acquired the premises of Beaven, Builders, in Dean Lane for a Mill and Timber Yard. They also obtained ground on the opposite side of the Lane to treat and store the trees. The trunks were brought to the Mill on trailers drawn by shire horses. While the Mill was full, the trees were stored on the other side of the Lane until required. In the Mill they were sawn into planks, stacked back on the trailer and moved to the other side of the Lane by the horses. Strips of wood were evenly placed across each plank as the tree trunk was assembled back to its normal shape to allow the air to circulate and dry out the wood. The trees were lifted by gantries and stored along the back of the houses in Essex and Catherine Mead Streets. Large iron gates where placed diagonally where Essex and Herbert Streets met to protect the area. Although lorries were used for transport in the 1930s, Clark's still worked the horses in the compound.

In 1909 the coalmines were closed and children gathered in the area to play. They looked for bits of china and glass in the rubble and shingle left from the dismantling of the mines. Parts of bricks were used to build little walls and separate their own little area. Hours of amusement must have been spent by the children, which inspired Dame Emily Smyth to give the ground as a play park in 1910. Shaddock's window cleaners lived in 'Chatham' cottage from 1925, and owned a yard known as Shaddock's Yard, which was situated in front of their cottage and next to St Paul's School. Access to their cottage was by a lane which ran along the side of Clark's Timber works. All their equipment for the window cleaning was kept in the yard. Contract cleaners, they kept all the shop windows clean, and could be seen at a great height on a platform worked by pulleys, cleaning the windows of Wills Factory. Mr. Edward James, living at No. 21 Dean Lane, 1920/1930s, owned a milk round. He didn't have transport, but with the help of a yoke he carried two small churns of milk to serve his customers.

Bristol South Baths

The Bristol South Baths were opened in 1933. Rules were lax at the beginning regarding time allowed and the number let in at any one session. Children could go on a Saturday morning from nine till noon for 1d. At times the shallow end was so crowded it was impossible to swim, but fun was still had by all.

Coronation Road

Coronation Road was so named after the Coronation of George IV in 1820. The other roads lining the New Cut also have royal connections, ie Clarence Road after the Duke of Clarence, third son of George III, Cumberland Road after the Duke of Cumberland's fifth son, York Road after the Duke of York, second son of George III. By 1820 Coronation Road was virtually completed. Long before the New Cut was excavated the area was called Bedminster Meadows. Facing Brandon Hill was Perry Hill, not the road now known as Upper Perry Hill, but a lengthy broad expanse of land, equal in height to Brandon Hill. Upon this hill a large part of Southville was developed over quite a long period with Coronation Road, Dean Lane and Alpha Road being the earliest.

Coronation Road was opened with a great deal of ceremony on the 23rd April 1822, and contemporary reports state that the Dowager Lady Smyth of Clift House, in a coach and four preceded by Captain Smyth's troop of Yeomanry, took part in the inaugural ceremony. The 1820s was a time of great expansion of middle class housing, but many of the merchants preferred the airy suburbs of Cotham, Redland and of course Clifton. But the area close to the New Cut, named at about this time Southville, became popular with artisans, seafaring men and generally people making their way in the world, as opposed to the poorer labouring classes of Bedminster.

The new Church of St Paul's was proposed in 1827 and an appeal was made to the public of Bedminster for funds to start the new church. Felix Farley's Journal reports that John Hare, who built Zion Chapel, gave 2 acres of land with frontage of about 200ft. The church was erected in 1829. Substantial houses were built around the Church and in Felix Farley's Journal in 1828 there is advertised the sale of two substantial newly-built villas on land belonging to John Acraman, part of a well-known Bristol company of Iron Founders. They later started a shipyard at the Clift House end of Coronation Road.

People of all ages had been falling into The Cut since it was first built. The early railings were flimsy and inadequate. Alderman Proctor took this matter in hand and by 1873 was building 'Proctor's Walk' on The Cut. His team cleared out weeds and bushes grown over sixty years and put in trees along the banks and along the pavement of Coronation Road. He also put up railings and good benches for people to enjoy the views. Some of these fruit and ornamental trees can still be seen amongst the ragged jumble of today from below Vauxhall Bridge to Bedminster Bridge, as can the stone built outlooks, which are too dangerous today to venture out upon. This admirable venture, which cost £500, was not appreciated by Chronicler Latimer who wrote, "a foolish attempt has been made to style this parade a 'Boulevard', but the public declined to adopt this misnomer." Latimer was incorrect in this case for Coronation Road continued to be used as a 'Boulevard' for over sixty years.

Road accidents too were occurring on Coronation Road. In Felix Farley's Journal of 10th January 1829, there is a report of a Mr Wm. Williams Snr. returning home from the country in his gig at about six o'clock in the evening, "when the horse, from some unknown cause, became restive and ran away along Coronation Road, and the evening being dark, the gig came in contact with a cart, and Mr Williams was thrown a considerable distance on the road, from which he had two broken ribs, and is otherwise much bruised. He is now lying in a very dangerous state".

By 1851 Matthews Directory shows a considerable number of people living on and near Coronation Road, including Mr. Manoah Williams of Hanover Villa, who was Master of the Commercial Rooms, a Mr. W Warcup a Civil Engineer at Lyndhurst Villa, a Ladies School at Bedford House run by the Misses Escott, several accountants, a ship owner and numerous sea Captains, so it was obviously a very desirable area to live. There was a large house on the corner of West End where a petrol filling station now stands. It was a lovely house with gardens and tennis courts. This was once owned by a dentist named Mr. Smith who lived there with his wife and daughter, Roma. The houses on the lower part of Coronation Road towards Ashton did not go up until after Vauxhall Bridge was built in 1900. By then several Off Licences appeared and more shops. The Post Office, once on the corner of Greenway Bush Lane had opened in 1890. As the 1930s rushed in, Coronation Road continued in quiet respectability, still a place of clergy, doctors, sea captains and schools, despite a pawnbrokers and barber's shop and a large garage being constructed.

Monty Maxfield said that the Coronation Road of the late 1920s was immaculately kept. The railings were painted and re-painted, weeds kept under control, any brass accessories on houses were highly polished and the entire road was still an important promenade. Boats still sailed down The Cut until the late 1930s. The *Isabella* was the last to be seen.

The Drum and Fife Band of the 16th Boy Scout Troop parading along Coronation Road in the late 1920s.

Merrywood Road

Merrywood Road was originally called Bull Lane, which dated back to ancient times. It was a place of orchards and farms and ran from North Street to the River Avon. Cattle were unloaded and slaughtered in the nearby vicinity, hence the origins of the name.

In the 1860s tradesmen began to build and Bull Lane was re-named Merrywood Lane and later Merrywood Road. The houses were re-numbered although some had names to distinguish one from the other. Aldred Collard became involved with house building at the lower end of Merrywood Lane. He had done a fair amount of travelling and it was known in his circle that he placed a huge variety of foreign coins under the foundations of the first house he built. In 1874 Collard was living in the corner shop at the bottom of Merrywood Lane, which he named Enmore House after his home village. His favourite pastime was reading poetry and being something of a poet himself, he erected the gargoyle with the inscription Poet's Corner 1882 over his corner shop. The premises were used at one time as a meeting place for miners. Collard had several shops on Redcliffe Hill and, in tribute to them, put Redcliffe House over the front door of 19 Merrywood Lane, where he lived in 1886.

Poets corner build in 1882, on the corner of North Street and Merrywood Road.

In 1900 Merrywood Lane was completely re-built and renamed Merrywood Road. It was re-numbered from North Street to Stackpool Road. Between 1905 and 1915 an assortment of businesses were operating in the road, amongst them a furniture dealer, a French Polisher, a dressmaker, a carpenter and joiner, a greengrocer and dairy, a timber merchant, a bootmaker and a hardware store. In 1915 at No 63 Miss Eliza Holbrook continued to run the corner shop with the help of her sister, gradually changing the trade to a General Store. The shop was frequently used by the school children who purchased blue tissue paper at a farthing a sheet and other items in the haberdashery line for their needlework lessons. The confectionery drew many of the children too, a favourite being of the half-penny 'everlasting strip'. Near the 5th of November festival, harmless fireworks and sparklers could be purchased. The two maiden ladies who ran the shop dressed always in black. They walked silently through the long passage from their living quarters, giving the shop an eerie atmosphere when they appeared. When farthings were in short supply, they gave their customers pins for change! At one time No 11 was occupied by Charles Warbutton, Confectioner. His shop was renowned for home-made Everton Toffee. Toffee apples were also sold. They were made in the family sweet factory at the rear of Lloyds Bank in East Street. The entrance was by way of Norfolk Place, the small lane at the side of the bank.

Merrywood Hall

Merrywood Hall was the only large mansion in Southville at the turn of the nineteenth century. It stood at the top of Bull Lane (Merrywood Road) with views from every aspect. Although few deeds exist, it is known that the Hall was built by the powerful and prestigious Powell family.

The Hall was the location for many important meetings, some of the most crucial concerned the future district church and the New Cut. Olcher Feddon was a voice at such meetings and he bought the property in 1832. He died there, suddenly, in 1839. The property was advertised to let in the Bristol Journal, "with hot house, pinery, greenhouse and garden, laid out in the first style" and "well calculated for a family of respectability." The advertisement neglected to mention the alleged ghost or ghosts of the Hall. Some say that the house was built on an ancient burial ground. There is no evidence for this, but few people were at ease in the building and many would not stay there at all. Certainly the Feddon relatives chose to move away.

The brilliant engineer Samuel Hemming bought the Hall in 1840 and lived there until 1856. Guests vied to attend the inaugural service for his iron church on Coronation Road and pressed to seek him out at home. By 1850 the cream of Southville society had crowded into Merrywood Hall and the wine cellars needed continual replenishment. In 1847 a new residence was built in Bull Lane adjoining the Hall. This was Merrywood Villa. Some documents refer to it as Merryfield Hall or Merrifield Villa - and others call it Merrywood Hall, which has, of course, caused confusion. This house was built by the Gore-Langtons. It is described in an 1850 Guide Book by John Morgan.....

Murryfield Hall (recently built) near St Paul's Church, Coronation Road, Bedminster, a beautiful and elevated spot, which directly fronts Clifton and Brandon Hill. Attached to this mansion in a fine orchard and garden, well stocked with wall fruit trees, adjoining to which was Merrywood Hall . . . From these mansions was a pleasant green field walk to Turnpike Gate, leading to Ashton and Leigh Woods.

In 1856 Hemming left Merrywood Hall in order to spend more time at his Bow Street, London, factory. The Hall, "with coach houses, stables, outhouses, cottage, yard, garden and premises extending to two acres" was sold to George Shadsworth Ogilvie, a surgeon with a private asylum in Eastville. Ogilvie transferred the asylum to Merrywood Hall. The 1861 census lists six 'scholars' living at the Hall, so it may also have operated as a private school.Mr Sims, whose grandmother lived nearby on Coronation Road in 1860, was told as a child about patients at the Hall peeping over the very high wall. It can only be imagined what actually went on there. In 1858 George Ogilvie had sold the veins and seams of coal lying under the Hall to the Bedminster Coal Company, headed by Henry Bennett. Bennett bought the Hall in 1862. Ogilvie does not appear to have moved immediately, though in 1867 he turned up in Redland and died the following year. He is buried in Southville in St Paul's graveyard. The Bennett family continued to live at the Hall until 1874. During these years more than one family lived at the Hall, and it was very crowded. By 1876 Merrywood Hall was in the possession of Anthony Tavener, Master Mariner, who had previously lived at Palma Villa, Dean Lane.

He did not like living at the Hall and returned quickly to his villa. The Hall was then sold to the Latham family. Latham, who was born in Bedminster, had made his fortune as a leather merchant at Redcliffe. With his family, he was determined to restore Merrywood Hall to all its former glory. Gardeners and stable keepers were set to work, painters and decorators refurbished the great house and the Latham girls, well-schooled in music and languages, set the place aglow with singing and piano playing. Mrs. Lily Gardner of Stackpool Road remembers Merrywood Hall as a 'gloomy place'. It had a high wall around it, ten feet, so it was difficult to see over it ... "Mr Latham was a very good and kind man, but behind those high walls the family was detached from us."

Latham died in 1906 and the Hall and site was purchased by Bristol Corporation. The buildings were demolished to make way for the new Merrywood Infant School in 1908. Merrywood Villa also went tumbling down. Demolition contractors, builders and local people were anxious to obtain stones, wooden adornments and hangings from the old Hall. Local tradition has it that the Hall's ghosts, too, went travelling on, and many claim that they have seen ghosts in certain parts of Southville.

This chapter presents the only factual research on Merrywood Hall ever attempted. The Southville History Group hopes that the memory and not just the ghosts of this great Southville house will forever endure!

This photograph of Merrywood Hall, although of poor quality is included because no other photograph of this building has come to light during research.

The New Cut

Contemporary reports of working on the New Cut seem almost non-existent but a little known book written by J P Malcolm, titled *Malcolm's First Impressions* telling of several travels he made in England between 1802 and 1805, tells of his visit to Bristol in June 1805. It gives a most interesting description of conditions in the City at the time, and also a first hand account of actual working on the New Cut, the effects of using gunpowder and also how the rocks loosened in the explosion were removed from the new excavation.

The New Cut looking down river, St Paul's Church on the left. The gatehouse of the old gaol can be seen on the right.

Starting on an excursion to Dundry, he says, "I crossed the Avon at the Gibb, at low water, and observed that the boat was pushed with a pole applied to the bottom of the river. The stream did not then appear to be more than four times the boat's length in breadth; and a large ship, the 'Mermaid' of New York, lay at a wharf, with her stern towards Redcliffe, full seven feet deep in the soft mud, by which the vessel was supported erect, as if water-borne, ten feet above the water. An unpleasant lane leads from the ferry to the verge of the new canal. As I passed this, a labourer advanced, and requested that I should return, as a person had at that instant fired the train of a ball of gunpowder, by means of which the workmen loosen the otherwise immovable rocks of the site. In that instant the explosion occurred, and I saw a thousand splinters of various sizes hurled into the air, that as instantaneously fell, in a dangerous shower, in a circle probably 400 feet in diameter."

Malcolm writes that the shock had not only rifted the rock immediately surrounding the powder, but huge fragments were removed from their beds, where wedges were driven into them. In this way they were made small enough to be raised with cranes by four men into carts which were conveyed up the banks by the operation of steam-engines erected on the verge of the canal. The engines turned several wheels with strong chains round them which by their revolutions lowered, emptied and raised the filled carts attached to the chains.

The writer describes the variety of strata in the canal between the Bath Road and Rownham Meads as 'highly interesting', consisting of fine sand, a lead-coloured clay and some gravel. He writes that "The excavation made through the rocks, though attended with great difficulty, has saved the proprietors a very considerable sum, as the stone was immediately used for the walls of the canal; and indeed this rock, cut perpendicular, serves as a wall for at least one quarter of a mile. The sand is admirably calculated for mixing mortar; and the company had merely to burn their lime, which they were preparing to do on the spot when I saw the works. A temporary bridge erected with the stone and intended mortar, crossed the canal at that time, but the fierce red of the sand in the latter ruined the appearance of the work. Iron bridges, are however, to be exclusively preferred."

Unfortunately Malcolm gives no indication where this temporary bridge was. As he makes no mention of having to walk any distance one can only infer that it would be between the end of Guinea Street, near the site of the General Hospital, the opposite end of the Gibb Ferry, close by the Ostrich Inn and Bedminster Bridge. This is the first indication of there being a temporary bridge across the excavations.

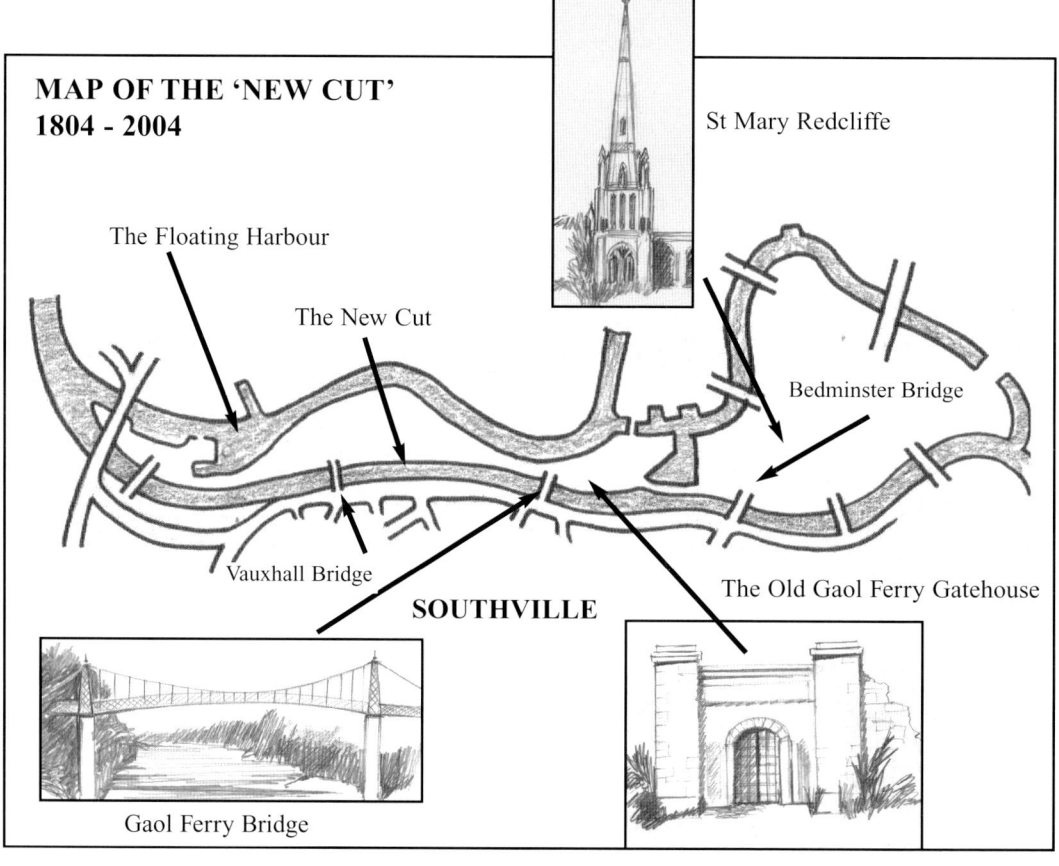

SOUTHVILLE CHURCHES

Southville's own Methodist Church originated in a Methodist meeting held in a house in St Thomas Street, Redcliffe; this later grew into the Portwall Lane Free Methodist Church, which was opened in 1859. This Chapel was sold in 1891 and the Methodist Society started meetings in a loft in Edgeware Road, Southville in the same year. These continued for about a year. Sites for a new chapel were considered and the present site in Stackpool Road was chosen. The chapel was opened on 11th January 1893, and the opening sermon was preached by the Rev. Henry Livesey.

Not all churches started in big purpose built buildings. When John Wesley preached in the Paddock (situated roughly at the back of the Wills Factory in East Street) it was the beginning of the Wesleyan Movement in the area. The first meetings were held in a house near Cannon Street, and later in a temporary building in Sheene Road. This building was donated by Mr Morgan, a local landowner. As congregations and collections increased plans were made to erect a church. Land in Back Lane (British Road) was purchased and the Wesleyan Chapel (later Ebenezer Church) was opened in 1837. Although this church, along with Hebron Chapel, East Street Baptist and Philip Street Baptist were not actually in Southville, they cannot be ignored because so many Southville residents attended them. Families sometimes separated on Sunday mornings or evenings and went to the church of their choice. Even married couples were known to disagree on this subject, one attending church and the other chapel. Some of the children of such marriages were baptised in church, some in chapel.

Holy Cross Roman Catholic Church, Dean Lane, opened in 1922.

The main chapel of the Open Brethren Movement was Bethesda Chapel, Clifton; this was too far for Southville people to walk, so the home of Mr H J Harris of 29 Leighton Road was used for prayer and Bible Study meetings in the early 1870s. In 1875 the Conservative Hall was rented for Sunday worship and by 1877 the Brethren had moved to the Temperance Hall, East Street, where a Sunday school was started. Weekly evening meetings were held in Dean Lane coal yard. Membership in 1881 was 188. In 1889 land in Merrywood Road was bought from Sir Hugh Smyth to build a chapel - the Gospel Hall. The land and the building of the Chapel cost £1,500, a Mr John Cordeaux putting up two-thirds of the cost.

Many local people attended the Gospel Hall services. It was particularly popular with children. Among those many children was Elsie Everitt (nee Garland) who remembers the Monday night services between the years 1906 -1913. The service consisted of the vigorous singing of hymns and a talk given by Mr Harris assisted by Mr Thomas. The chapel would be full of children, not always on their best behaviour. The most popular nights were when there was a magic lantern show. To those children born before television or even the 'wireless', it really was magical. The service nearest to Christmas Day was marked by each child being given an orange as they left. The Sunday school held during the afternoon was also well attended; each class was partitioned off by curtains. For many years opposite the chapel was a little sweet shop and on Monday nights this shop was besieged by children spending their farthings and ha'pennies before they went into the service.

By the 1900s St Paul's church was the dominant force in Southville. It provided various social activities for the adults and at the same time over 2,000 benefited from its sponsored Day School and Sunday School classes. Southville at this time was an area of two classes - the upper classes lived in the large properties of Stackpool, Coronation and Acramans Roads, whilst the lower classes lived in the small terraced working area characterised by the Dean Lane Pit, although work was scarce and many families lived in poverty. The church arranged various societies and organizations, some of which were specifically to help the poor. These included: The Barnabas Society, which provided various articles for the sick room, such as feeding cups, airbeds and chairs; The Blanket Lending Society, which loaned blankets to the poor; The Children's Help Society, which during cold weather provided half-penny dinners for poor children. Other church organizations were the Clothing Club, the Band of Hope and various Bible Classes. These were held at the Mission House, the Church Vestry and Dean Lane School.

St Paul's had its own District Visitors, who visited the poor and sick of the Parish, also a Library in the Mission Hall. There was also the St Paul's Lawn Tennis and Cricket Club, which is still in existence as the Bedminster Cricket Club. It was formed in 1847 and was for some years based at Luckwell Lane, where W G Grace made his first public appearance in a match between Bedminster and Swindon. On leaving Luckwell Lane a move was made to a ground now occupied by Wills in Raleigh Road and in 1898 the Club moved again to a ground at Ashton Gate. At the time of writing the club's ground is at The Clanage, Bower Ashton.

The Salvation Army was not to be left out. It organised what it called 'Slum Posts' to help the poor and needy. The Salvation Army is probably best remembered for its Band. During the 1930s it played every Saturday night in the East Street area. The Band was so popular with the late night shoppers that the crowds caused traffic congestion. The shopkeepers complained to the Police, who tried to stop the playing, but there was such an outcry from local people, that the Band was allowed to carry on playing in the area until the outbreak of the War. The Salvation Army Band's boast was that it had played or marched through every street in Bedminster.

The Salvation Army church. Two of the foundation stones were laid by Lady Emily F Smyth of Ashton Court and Mrs. C E Gibbs of Tyntesfield House, in 1909. It will be noted that although it has been customary to end the Smyth family name with an 'e', the family itself were content to do with out it.

'Southville Beau'

'Southville Beau' was a small Yorkshire terrier, bred and owned by Mr Charles and Mrs Laura Burge of 49 Langton Park, Southville. During the 1914 - 1918 War he collected over 10,000 pennies for the Soldiers and Sailors Wool Fund. Mrs Burge knitted 'Southville Beau' a suit of red, white and blue. A box with a Union Jack, toy soldiers and a toy gun was fixed to his back and he was taken out to collect money. Mr. Burge worked for the Bristol Tramway Co. and his favourite collecting spots were at the top of Redcliffe Street where trams stopped and at the London Inn. The little dog was small enough to be held in one hand. He would be held up by Mr Burge so that the people on the top deck of the tram could contribute. When the dog died it was stuffed and kept on the sideboard in the Burge home. It remained there until the mid 1930s.

WOMEN

Southville women wielded a strong influence on the growth of the community. In the 1840s two women, Mrs Elizabeth Acraman and Mrs E Morgan were property owners. Anne Day and Ann Hort were important occupiers of Southville land.

Martha Wakefield, the official Southville Scavenger in 1851, lived in Dean Lane and had a farm in North Street. Being very powerful and rich Mrs Wakefield was haughtily unconcerned about people's opinions and was one of Southville's most outrageous ladies. Her home at Somerset Cottage, Dean Lane, was amongst the elite of Southville and whilst her neighbours may not have been delighted by her presence, they were not anxious to provoke her. Other early women appeared to skirt under the tailcoats of menfolk whilst being the power behind them. Most followed feminine pursuits and were the backbone of the Church and Family. A few were individualists. In the 1840s the organist of St Paul's was a woman. We do not know her name but we know of her existence from the writings of Joseph Leech, the 'Church Go-er' of the Bristol Times. He wrote that this woman organist was "probably the first in Bristol".

Mary Wilcox or Baker, the Princess Caraboo of Javasu, was another of Southville's renowned women. The Princess first appeared in Bristol in 1817 as a prestigious East Indian Princess. Important personages did homage to her until her ruse was discovered. We believe she was twelve or even younger when she carried off her impersonation as a foreign princess. In the 1820s she was sent to Knowle to a mental institution. In the 1840s she lived in Southville. Two Mary Bakers are recorded in the 1851 Census. Both lived in Southville, are the same age and have two children. Both have a daughter of the same age and the same name. Obviously they are one woman with two addresses. Certainly the Princess married a Mr Baker of Southville and had two children. In later years, the daughter of the Princess took the name of Mary Baker. It is thought, but not proved, that Baker was a local policeman.

For a while Princess Caraboo settled down to domesticity and motherhood, but was unable to sustain conventional behaviour. In the 1850s she became a leech collector in

Mary Wilcox, alias 'Caraboo, Princess of Javasu.'

the local Malago stream. Many Southville streets claim her as a resident but her longest stay appears to have been in Old Charlotte Street, close by the Malago. The Princess was buried at Hebron Chapel in 1865. In the Church register she is described as Mrs Baker (princess). The fact that she was buried at Hebron Chapel substantiates the fact that Mr Baker was a respected Southville citizen. The daughter, Mary Baker, continued her mother's occupation as a leech gatherer and wandered around Southville. Few facts exist about the daughter and many stories about her and the princess are intertwined, because they have the same name. She was buried at Arnos Vale in the 1880s.

Southville women successfully ran Public Houses. The 1801 Census designates Elizabeth Clark as owning the 'Hen & Chicken' on North Street and Jane Powell as owner of the 'Masons Arms' on the same road. Mary Howell and Sarah Owen were turnpike keepers in Bedminster. However this job was a sinecure. Women also ran shops, but mostly in the grocery and haberdashery businesses. A few were pork butchers, usually a male prerogative, and one women on North Street was a lath plasterer.

From the early 1800s women had done the hardest and most poorly paid jobs in the tanneries, glue and ironwork factories on Coronation Road and in the Southville roads at the back of East Street. When Wills and Robinsons opened in East Street in the 1880s, working women were much more valued. Those of more affluent or conservative families continued to put their considerable energies into the Church in the 1880s and 1890s, as Southville grew. The deepening issue of Women's Suffrage kept Southville, if not exactly boiling, stirring. The Bedminster Industrial Co-operative Society had premises in Dean Street in 1886 and women were stalwarts of the society. In 1899 Mrs Emily Gough of Southville was listed as one of the 'Committee Men'. By 1901 three women were elected to the Committee of the Bedminster Society. The Women's Guild started in the early 1890s and were spurred on to independence by visits of well know suffragette leaders to Dean Street.

Mrs Gough, who became Vice President of the Bedminster Women's Guild as well as Treasurer and Secretary, lived at Portland House, Milford Street, before moving to Merrywood Road in 1900. She encouraged education in Southville and gave many local lectures on employment and social affairs. Her profession was 'seamstress and mantle maker'. Other local supporters of the Women's Guild and Suffrage were Miss Edith Evans of 66 Stackpool Road; Mrs Anne Andrews of Milford Street; Mrs Morgan, Mrs Rider and Mrs Martin of Coronation Road. Miss Evans had been elected a Bristol Guardian of the Poor in the early 1890s and ran again in 1898 against the local vicar. There were three Guardian Boards in Bristol. The Southville-Bedminster Board was a hotly contested political office made up of well known people to ensure that the poor, unemployed and under-privileged were given their dues under the law. She was a powerful influence in Southville affairs.

Another staunch lady of Southville was Mrs. L Halliday, who lived at No 12 Ashton Gate Road (the North Street end of Greenway Bush Lane). Mrs. Halliday was one of the women to pass a resolution in favour of Women's Suffrage in 1896 and was the Secretary of Bedminster Women's Guild for many years. While Mrs. Halliday was somewhat isolated from the other Southville members of the group who lived in or close to Stackpool Road, she received valuable support from leading business women in Greenway Bush Lane like Mrs. Rebecca Thorne, who ran the Beaconsfield Club in that road. All these Southville women were active in the move to strengthen a woman's place in the workforce, especially with the building of the new Wills factories in Raleigh Road in 1900 and the subsequent building of many shops and businesses on North Street. Women were now 'allowed' to run newsagents and tobacco shops. The coming of World War 1 saw women accepted in most kinds of employment. Women ran their own small police force and patrols for working Southville women. But, after the War, there was a backlash. Jobs were needed by men and most women had no choice but to stay at home. They turned to traditional 'working from home' jobs: dressmaking, millinery, hairdressing, domestic work, childcare, sweet making and the keeping of shops.

Teachers of any kind were the most socially acceptable people, as were nurses and midwives, who all thrived in Southville. Women continued to lead the workforce of big businesses at Wills and Robinsons, but never in supervisory or managerial levels. They had achieved the right to vote but not to oversee men. By the early 1920s an urgent need for secretarial skills gave women an edge on competing in the business world. But most, it has to be said, used their skills to get a husband, as marriageable men were at a premium after the War. Over the years of the area's growth many able women chose or had no choice but to follow the prostitution trade and there were several 'hospitable houses' in the area.

Many women were betting runners. Putting a 'bob' (5p) or two on the horses or football was a very popular pastime but this was illegal until the 1960s. So women, especially housewives, played a major role in this underground activity. It was simple for women with their daily shopping and social habits, to combine this with running or passing bets. One woman of Catherine Mead Street was a bookmaker.

A few women went in for wrestling, which was a popular sport held at the back of Bedminster Hippodrome, close to Catherine Mead Street. Billy Price, a welter-weight boxer, who fought as a young man in the Bedminster Arcade in the early 1930s, told us about the women wrestlers who were cheered on by Southville folk on Saturdays. Price received £2 10s a fight. "I don't know how much the women got but it was certainly more than the men, because they had more on-lookers. It was a good show and definitely got my attention," he said. Some local women objected to this exhibition.

The women, of post World War 1 times continued to make slow gains. They were active in politics, particularly in the Liberal party. A few women made remarkable progress. The first female Bristol Auctioneer, Mrs. Cornett, was a Southville woman. She was the daughter of Thomas Smith, who had been a chemist at Sholto Place, between Myrtle and King William Street, on North Street in the 1890s. Mrs. Agnes Steward, Physician and Surgeon was practising at Beauley House before 1930 - the first of many women doctors to work in Southville.

Southville women were gathering strength before the burdens of World War II fell upon them.

LANDOWNERS

H G Fowler was the grandson of the extremely wealthy and powerful John Fowler, whose wealth had come from slavery. Henry George inherited his grandfather's deep interest in Southville. He wanted to develop the area and was among those who petitioned for the building of St Paul's church and attended the stone laying with his brother Richard. Henry Fowler had a business address of 137 Redcliffe Hill and was listed in Directories as 'merchant'. He had early established himself in the business community and was a member of the Chamber of Commerce and Trade (established January 1st 1823) and by 1833 was an 'assistant' at the Merchant Venturers Society. He was also Consul to France in 1833.

Deeds of old houses on Edgware, Pembroke, Osborne and Allington Roads have 'Fowlerville' listed rather than Southville. Arrowsmith's Map of 1886 has the name 'Fowlerville' instead of Allington Road. The first alphabetically listed landowner of Southville in 1845 was Elizabeth Acraman, widow of John Acraman. She owned the small, but important piece of land directly opposite St Paul's, number 160. She also had 161 adjoining 160 and facing onto Dean Lane. That land surrounding the Church, 192 and that behind it, 190, stood in the horseshoe of the original piece of land called SOUTHVILLE.

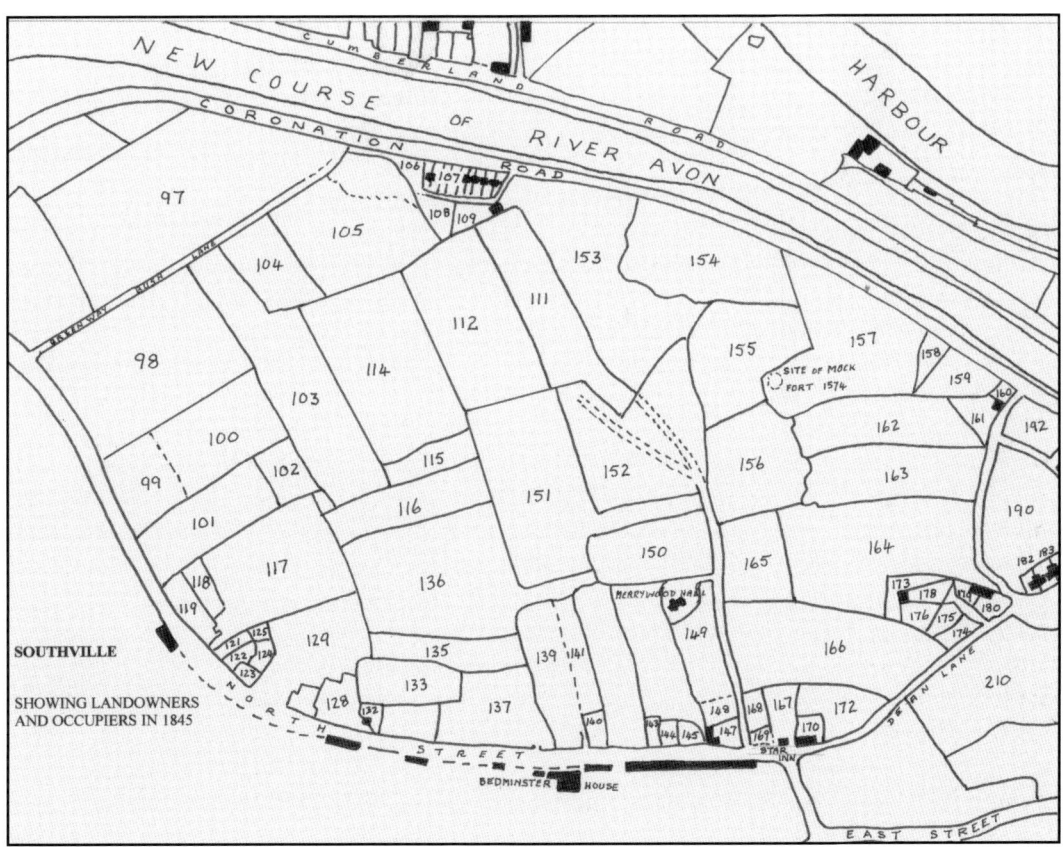

John Acraman, who was born in 1772, might well be called the founder of Southville. He had strongly urged for St Paul's to be built on his land rather than a plot being considered near Bath Bridge. The petition to the Bishop of Bath and Wells on March 5th 1828 was signed by him as well as other owners and occupiers of Southville land. Achieving his aim of seeing the Church planned, Acraman was present at the stone laying the following year. He was not particularly interested in St Paul's itself, since he was a member of Redcliffe Church and both he and his wife, Elizabeth are buried there. He was interested in the building of a district, which the establishment of a church would bring. A member of a large and powerful family with interests in shipping, iron manufacturing and imports, Acraman, who had known years before the actual course of the Cut, was keen to have his very own shipyard. There is no doubt that he originally intended the 'gaol ferry' as a shipyard. The construction, which can still be clearly seen below Gaol Ferry Foot Bridge is much too extensive for a ferry. He started to build the arched Coronation Bridge before 1819. It is engraved J A and dated July 19th 1821.

Acraman opened the ferry in the summer of 1828. This would be the most important crossing into Southville by boat until 1935. The Dock Company approved of this crossing and it remained the property of Elizabeth Acraman until 1854. Then it was transferred to the City Corporation upon payment to her of £200. Realising that the Cut opposite St Paul's was too narrow for extensive shipping activities, Acraman put his energy into the building of a shipyard near Vauxhall Ferry. Indeed, despite financial problems, this shipyard was built on the Cut only just before Acraman's death. Known as the Acraman-Payne's shipyard it built and repaired ships until 1924. It is only the 'Neptune' (built at Bideford in 1811) that was positively owned by John Acraman, together with Thomas King. Both are described as 'merchants and West India men of Bristol.'

Acraman was a member of the Suspension Bridge company formed in 1830. One of his chief talents was the formulation of the important projects. The Cut had been his most ambitious undertaking. He did not live to see this later scheme realised, but then neither did he live to see the Acraman family ruined by bankruptcy. By 1841 the Acraman family were in deep financial trouble. On July 7th 1845, Harford & Coy. became official assignees of the estate and effects of Messrs D E & A Acraman. They were bankrupt and the Acraman family faded away.

Acraman was a man of driving ambition and ruthlessness. Even though he had petitioned so ardently for a House of God to be built on his land, the year before he had let a man (and, say some reports, a child also) be sentenced to the treadmill for two months. The crime was stealing a few pieces of fruit from the orchards of this very same site on Dean Lane. Such attitude was a part of the age in which he lived. The great achievement of John Acraman to our history is his powerful impetus to the development of Southville. Acraman's Road is a reminder of his acheivements. His original ferry crossing can still be seen today below The Gaol Ferry Bridge which replaced the service and remains the main foot crossing into Southville today.

Thomas Pym was the main occupier of the Acraman land. He occupied parcels 160, 161 and 192. Plot 160 is described as a garden, outhouses and yard. 161 is described as two cottages and gardens and 192 as a nursery. Lots 160 and 192 are the Acraman properties with access to the New Cut and thus Coronation Road. Pym is named in the 1842 (Mathews) Directory as a Florist, operating the Southville Tea Gardens on Coronation Road. They are likely to have been opposite the Church. Pym's tea gardens flourished for a short time and were popular with sermon-parched visitors!

The 1820 Directory lists Mr Hutchings as a Chairmaker at the Star Inn. There, Hutchings would have been in close contact with Thomas Hassell who presided at the Bedminster Sessions held at the Star. Hutchings perhaps made the Magistrate's chair. In the accounts of the Bristol Riots of 1831 (to be found at Bristol Reference Library), William Humphries was Governor of the New Gaol, and Hassell was one of those presiding at the Appeal Court Session held in January 1832. Humphries had put in a claim for loss of goods from the partial destruction of the Gaol and this included a considerable amount of furniture. He received money for the claim. The fact that he was not at the Gaol at the time of the riots and the claim itself, did not endear him to the authorities. Further, his testimony against local accused man William Clarke, in contrast to that of many Bedminster and Southville trades folk and members of St Paul's, made Humphries extremely unpopular. For a time he ran the Star with James Martin and occupied adjacent land on Dean Lane. (This plot 172 belonged to Smythe). He is listed in the 1846 Directory as living at 11 Ashton Terrace on Coronation Road. This terrace was close by St Paul's. Almost thirty years later, in 1872, Mrs. Sarah Humphries, the widow of William, was still living at this address.

Joseph Cottle, publisher and poet is Southville's most renowned resident. His publication of the then unknown poets, Robert Southey, Samuel Coleridge, Charles Lamb and William Wordsworth, made Cottle famous throughout the country in literary circles. He had encouraged the young poets in Bristol with both money and support. Cottle moved from the City to Southville in 1832 to a newly built gracious house at Carlton Terrace at the top of North Street. It was in this area of Southville that Cottle entertained the Poet Laureate Robert Southey in 1836. It was also here that he wrote several books of his own, including the controversial book about Samuel Coleridge, to whom he had been close some years before.

We cannot limit our story of Cottle to his Southville years, since he so clearly knew the area very well from the end of the 18th Century. In October 1795 Cottle and his sister Sarah attended the Redcliffe Church wedding of Coleridge to Sarah Fricker, who lived with her mother and sisters on Redcliffe Hill. The following month, Cottle not only attended the wedding of Southey to Sarah's sister, Edith Fricker, but also supplied the ring. Cottle would have known Southey's Bedminster relatives and attempted to get assistance from them for the destitute poet. Although it has to be said that Joseph Cottle was not a very good poet himself, his natural enthusiasm, constant encouragement and generosity to the famous writers and poets who were his friends, are testaments to the wealth of his spirit.

Samuel Hemming is the next landowner having Lot 150 in Southville. This lot is a prime area with orchards, fields and a house. Bull Lane (Merrywood Road) ran right past Hemming's property. There would have been a direct route to the lower end of Coronation Road where Hemming had his business. He built the very first pre-fabs at Vauxhall Yard. While many were experimenting with galvanized iron buildings, Hemmings was particularly innovative.

He made houses, shops and even churches. It was on Coronation Road that a special service was held in a church he had built for Melbourne. This was conducted by the Bishop of Melbourne assisted by local clergy on May 13th 1853. Tickets were issued for the 800 important people who attended the service. The event received extensive press coverage, both locally and in the *Illustrated London News.*

Thomas Hort, a butcher, is the next landowner. In 1851 he was seventy-seven and lived with his wife Jane and various female relatives at Carlton Place. Lots 123 and 135 were owned by Hort. The first was a small plot on North Street which appears to have been a small row of shops roughly where they are today, by King William Street. Hort himself had a butcher's shop there, although his main shop had previously been on Redcliffe Hill. He had been a butcher since the later years of the 18th century and had known his neighbour Joseph Cottle for many years. His other Lot was a large field at the back of North Street and here, in view of his occupation, he kept livestock. This area was close to the main Hort home and Elizabeth Morgan kept cattle here. Arthur Smith, a bacon factor, occupied Lots 128 and 131, directly on North Street. He had a shop here and lived either above it or in the next building. Smith also had gardens and a building, where he cured his bacon.

Elizabeth Morgan, owner of this land, chose to live on Cannon Street, where she had lived for many years with her husband John. John Morgan had made a fortune from butchering and with his money he helped others in founding churches. He had shown particular generosity to local Methodists, providing meeting rooms for them at Eldon Cottage, where his widow lived in 1845. Earlier Morgan furnished Methodists with another meeting room in his warehouse in Shim Lane (Sheene Road) Bedminster. Then in 1828, in company with his friend and fellow butcher, William Hort, he had pressed for the building of St Paul's in Southville. John Fuller is listed in directories of the time as a 'Gentleman'. He is noteworthy for owning the smallest parcel of land in the Southville of 1845. It was Lot number 124, which lay between those owned by Hort and Cottle. They all lived at Carlton Place. Fuller owned a house and gardens. It does not seem he was married or involved in very much, other than being a gentleman. Surrounded by women at Carlton Place, it is hoped he enjoyed poetry, music and good food.

We deal now with the property owned by the established Church, but only one Lot concerns us, number 95, as the rest of the land was at Ashton. Thomas Merlove was the lessee for St Paul's and he leased it to John Thayer and Henry Wildgoose.

Wildgoose is listed in 1839 as owning a brickyard at 1 Coronation Buildings, Coronation Road. In May of that year, Police Occurrence books state that Wildgoose's white drake with a green bell was stolen from this brickyard. No doubt the drake was kept to scare off intruders and had not done well at his work. Land directly off Greenway Bush Lane, behind the Avon Packet and adjoining buildings on Coronation Road, was leased by Wildgoose from Smyth. (Lot 105 - described as 'Field and Kilns'). In the Corporation Minute Books of May 1867, Wildgoose is mentioned as taking an apprentice from the Bedminster workhouse. Wildgoose is described as a 'Harrier.' The 1851 Census gives his age as 39, so he began his brickyard as a young man.

We come now to the considerable holdings of Sir John Smythe in Southville, held separately from that of Gore Langton. While all the occupants are interesting people, none captures the imagination as much as Samuel Clarke. He was born in 1791, the son of Jacob and Elizabeth Clarke. Jacob was Manager of the Hen and Chicken in 1797, but Elizabeth owned the Public House in 1801. Samuel is first mentioned in Directories as having a timber yard on Coronation Road in 1820. This was close to Harford's Bridge (Bedminster Bridge) and he also kept his accounting office at this address. His residence is also listed as the Hen and Chicken in North Street. He was a leading citizen of Southville and petitioned for St Paul's in 1828. He is listed as an occupier, but is most likely to have owned the land. We need here to mention once again that the spelling of almost all the names on the Tythe List varies from deed to deed and in accounts of the day.

It was not long after the opening of St Paul's that Samuel's life was to be scarred by tragedy. His nephew William had lived in Southville since 1817. When he was nine he had gone with his uncle to the sawmill on Coronation Road and there suffered a head injury. William Clarke was one of the scapegoats of the Bristol Riots. Unfortunately, the young man, then aged 22, had boasted of his part in the raiding and pillaging of the New Gaol, opposite Coronation Road. It also came out in evidence at the Trials that William had shown at the 'Hen and Chicken' what were said to be the keys of the Gaol. Clarke did all that was in his power to free his tragic nephew, assisted by other influential people in Bedminster and Southville. The Morgans, Stokes, Gissolds, James Cheese, George Gange and Thomas Trott all testified to the good character of Will Clarke. The Sheriff's men, who were the law in Southville, did their best to help Samuel Clarke. At the special hearing convened in January 1832 after pleas by both the Clarke family and Southville people, William Clarke lost his fight for life. Elizabeth Clarke, his mother, appeared at the hearing and when she was called, young Will fainted. Her appeals for clemency were ignored. It was vital for the government to have a 'victim.' Will Clarke, aged 22, was hanged on January 27th 1832, only thirteen days after the special trial. St Paul's churchyard was crowded to watch the execution of Clarke and three others chosen to be killed in the name of 'justice'. Samuel Clarke, who lived on Coronation Road at Wellington Terrace, would have been within sight of the Gaol and had good cause to drown his sorrows at this time. Clarke left Southville for a while, preferring to live in other districts. By the early 1840s he had returned to live at the 'Hen and Chicken' with his young wife Susan.

John Thayer occupied Deans Close, a long Lot lying directly off Dean Lane. In 1861 Thayer was 60 and still lived with his wife Esther at Deans Close. It is known that Thayer had shipping interests and that a relation, George Thayer, was a pilot for the 'Vigilant' in 1842.

In 1845, the Manor Lords technically owned two thirds of Southville land. Because of the financial pressures of the times on these Lords and because a lot of these old families were dying out, by 1845 many Lots, Fields and Houses had been sold. Sir John Smythe, a bachelor, was gone by 1849, and until Greville Upton became a Smythe by marriage and was created a baronet in 1859, there was some confusion about who owned what.

Martha Wakefield, who occupied Lot 113 'Northfield' was Southville's most zestful early lady. She was the official Scavenger for the area and was so appointed, together with Samuel Wakefield in 1851; one person's rubbish is a fortune for those willing to sift through it. Skinning and processing the many hides that passed through Southville was a lucrative business, but it was not perhaps one in which many ladies would have so actively and publicly participated in the mid 1800s. Martha Wakefield thought nothing of her notoriety and her name appears frequently in *Journals and Sanitary Complaints Minutes* of the times. In 1851 complaints of the smell from the Wakefield Yard are recorded. A police report of 1853 states that the Wakefields were charged with depositing loads of ashes at Dean Lane. The population of Southville, already stifled by the miasma from the Cut made constant complaints against the family. By the end of the 1880s the Wakefields seem to have tired of scavenging and established one of the first known shops in Stackpool Road. The shop which was later owned by the Brays at this location originally belonged to the Wakefields. In 1900 we have only Joseph Wakefield in our area at 13 Warden Road.

There were many tanneries in Southville and Bedminster and even today many people can recall the distinctive smell associated with this trade. A link with this trade survives in the manufactory of Thomas Ware & Son Ltd. at Ashton.

SCHOOLS

The 1870 Education Act was the first of a series of Acts of Parliament that was to eventually lead to all children being recipients of free education in schools administered by the Local Authority. Prior to the establishment of the new 'Board Schools' in Southville the education of children was provided by attending either a Private School or a Church School. Southville had both types of school.

The first recorded Private School, close to Southville, was situated in Clift House Road. This was prior to the construction of Coronation Road. The school was named 'Holt Brandt Seminary for Young Gentlemen'. During 1817, the school was taken over by William Goulstone and renamed 'Bedminster Boys Academy'. It was moved to North Street at the corner of what is now Hebron Road and although not in Southville itself, the owner was one of Southville's major landowner/occupiers, who held much property in the Dean Lane area. At the Academy, tuition was given in Latin, Greek and the Classics; Commercial and English Instruction was also taught. The annual charges were; thirty guineas for boarders, twenty-five guineas for weekly boarders and eighteen guineas for day pupils. There were extra charges for washing, books and stationery. Vacations were one month at Christmas and one month at mid-summer. For those children who could not go home for the holidays, there was a charge of five guineas per week, for accommodation.

William Goulstone was extremely active in getting St. Paul's built and his school band, with banners flying, were at the ceremony for the laying of the foundation stone. Other schools were also present, including Bedford House Academy, which was situated in a Georgian building in the newly constructed Coronation Road. In 1830, 'The Academy for Young Ladies', run by a Miss Townsend, was opened, also in Coronation Road. The charges at this school were twenty-two guineas for board and tuition in all branches of English education, twenty guineas for weekly boarders and four guineas for boarders and four guineas for daily pupils, who partook of breakfast and dinner. Latin, Greek, French and Drawing were taught at an extra charge of four guineas each; one quarter's notice or an equivalent payment was expected before the removal of a pupil. Holiday arrangements were the same as the Bedminster Boys Academy except that the charge was only two guineas. Bills had to be settled half yearly.

Some other early schools in the area were:-

1833	The ragged school in the basement of Zion Church, Coronation Rd.
Pre 1850	Mrs Jones Boarding School for Young Ladies at 9 Richmond Place, Coronation Rd, (near St. Paul's Church). Private.
1850	Mrs. G. Gilbert's Preparatory School for Young Ladies, Coronation Rd. Private.
1870	Mr. J. Newton's School, 1 Florence Place, Southville, (now covered by Asda car park) Private.
1870	Maria Everett Ladies School, 6, Richmond Place (moved in 1872 to 46, Southville Place) Private.
1872	Elizabeth Maies School, Dean Lane. Private.

1872	St. Paul's School, Dean Lane. (Built in mock Gothic style, it was demolished in 1959.
1877	Misses Frost and Fryer Ladies School, Coronation Villas. Private
1884	William Fox, (schoolmaster) Evans Villa, Stackpool Rd.
1885	Mrs Prescott Ladies School, Kemply House, Coronation Rd. Private.
1886	Mrs Kingdon Ladies School, 23 Stackpool Rd. Private.
1897	A special school for children with mental disabilities was founded at Zion Chapel. In 1903 it moved to Stillhouse Lane. The school provided accommodation for both boys and girls.

By 1896, there were three main schools in Southville. They were the Beauley Road Board School, St. Paul's School in Dean Lane and the Board School in Greenway Bush Lane. South Street School was close by as was the British School in British Road. Holy Cross School in Dean Lane did not open until 1912.

Southville Primary School (formerly Merrywood Schools)

With the kind permission of the Board of Governors of Southville Primary School we have taken a selection from the *Jubilee Southville Star Magazine* of 1958. Our choice is of the pre-World War 2 years, where possible. (It should be noted that this selection was made in 1987, ed.)

From
Miss E.M. Burnell:
'I am in the unique position of having spent the whole of my teaching career in this one school, having done my Teaching Practice as a college student, and returning later as a Qualified Teacher.'

As I look back on those early days I am reminded of the many, many times I crossed the water of the 'Cut' in the ferry-boat, long before the Goal Ferry Bridge was built. Older readers will remember the cheery personality of Mr. 'Dick' Thomas, who took us over for 1/2d toll.

The passing of the years brought many changes of all kinds - the introduction of the 'Milk in Schools' scheme, school dinners, etc. and a gradual change in school methods and organisation. I sometimes sigh for the days when children knew how to sit still and the classroom really was a quiet place.

I have recollections of countless children who spent their early years with us here, many of whom stand out in memory very clearly. It is with pride and pleasure that I hear of their achievements - some following in the steps of their teachers, two now serving in the Church of Christ, another, a successful artist, while another is making a name for herself in the world of theatre.

From Miss G. Knowles - Headmistress of St. Anne's Park Junior School (in 1958):

I remember, what shall I remember? So many incidents concerning Southville Primary School come crowding to my mind. The first day at school, when aged four and a half years, I came into Miss Thomas' class and sat wondering, open-eyed and eared, among fifty others. We sat solemnly in dual desks, each with a small box of wooden cubes in front of us. And yet, grim as this sounds, they were happy days full of interest and 'busy-ness.' I remember the first day as a teacher, when I entered the building with much more trepidation than before. Time had gone on, the fashion of learning changed,

Class 2 of Merrywood Senior School, taken not long after the school opened in 1908.

and now in front of me sat fifty-four - not so quiet seven year olds, all anxious to experiment with a new teacher. The time came for Miss C.E. Rowland to retire, and to mark the occasion she hired the Town Hall - then a cinema, and on a bitterly cold December afternoon we marched through the snow to enjoy a programme of films. It was quite an event, nearly all Southville watched us on our way.

From Miss D.K. Burrows, 1933-1939 (Member of Staff) - Headmistress of
Oake Primary School, Somerset (1958):

I remember a school with an entirely female staff under the organisation of a personality dedicated to make it 'an elementary school', plus. Meticulous speech and manners were expected from all. The aim was to surround the children with beauty of all kinds, including the beauty of well-written work, graceful movement, musical sounds, as well as artistically kept surroundings. No child ever addressed a mistress as Miss. The absolute and well kept rule fostered untiringly amongst the youngest Infants was a well-ingrained habit by Junior days. In my varied experience since, I have never seen it so successfully maintained. When Miss Walker came, she added a very human understanding to this well prepared 'ground.' I was very sorry when the strain of such a large school proved too much for her. The Staff, too, was composed of people whom one does not easily forget. Miss Wilkins of the Infant School and Miss Kirkland, so understanding of slower children, were our seniors; Miss Gliddon with her apt and dry sense of humour and in their pre-headships, Miss Edgar, Miss Jones and Miss Knowles.

From Miss E.K. Gay - on the Staff of Victoria Park School (1958):

In August 1916, I was appointed with another young lady to be a student teacher at Merrywood Junior Mixed and Infants' School. At that time there were ten classrooms, each, except the reception class, with two raised platforms running across so that the two back rows of desks could be seen. There were six Infant and four Junior classes each with fifty to sixty children.

In February 1919 I returned to the school as a trained Certified teacher. All staff were expected to 'sign on' by 8.40 a.m. At 8.50 a bell rang, when the children 'lined up' ready to march into school in two's, making a smart right-angle at the bottom of the hall, and another opposite the classroom. This happened again at 12 noon and 4.15 or 4.30 p.m. If the weather was bad, preventing play, the Headteacher played 6/8 music and each class in turn skipped once round the hall in double lines, the girls holding out their skirts as they skipped. The mornings were spent in Number, Reading, Writing and formal Physical Training. Even the five year olds were expected to be able to write two times table on squared paper with correct placing, leaving spaces for tens and units. Reading was taken by the whole class reading from the same book. I can remember one book which said, 'I am an ox. An ox is by me.' Children who did careless or poor work, or who lost their places in reading were kept in after school. No teacher left her room until 12.30 or 12.45 p.m. No dinners were served nor milk provided. Every term the Headteacher spent two days in each room examining the class and writing a report on all subjects. Most terms the local Inspector came to examine the school and every term registration was checked. For many years we had Mr. Bingham who banged every door loudly, a warning I used to think, in case one had not closed the register. On Friday afternoons all the staff had to stay to take register totals and percentages to the Head's desk in the hall. Our holidays were one month in the summer, two days at half-term (Teachers' Rest!), about a fortnight at Christmas, ten days at Easter and seven at Whitsuntide.

From Evan L. Shroll (1908) (Written 1958):
Fifty years ago, when I was eight years old, I came to Southville Primary School, or as it was known then, Merrywood Infants School, on the very day it was opened. I well remember the smell of new paint everywhere and perhaps it was the freshness of everything which inspired me to try to be the best pupil in my class.

From Mrs. M.E. Shute :

It is interesting to recall that Southville Primary School was built on the site of a large house, standing in its own grounds, called Merrywood Hall, the only surviving part of which is the tree to be seen in the playground facing Merrywood Road. In 1908 the school was opened under the name of Merrywood Junior School a fitting title, bearing in mind its association with the past.

Ever since then, progress has been the watchword and for half a century a high standard in education and principles have been maintained. It is still a joy to me to know that my children and grandchildren started their school life here in a happy atmosphere, and with a teaching staff whose child psychology formed such an important background. In 1930 a team of eleven pupils in the top class won a handwriting contest open to the United Kingdom, a shield was presented by Messrs. Harrod of London. This was really a commendable feat, the shield being won from a Scottish school. Certificates were presented to each member of the team, one of my daughters being a recipient.

From Mrs. M. Archer
Southville 25 Years Ago (1933):

The first and most striking change is in the name of the school, as Southville Primary School was then called Merrywood Junior School. School life seemed to be rather more serious than today as swimming and outside visits were considered privileges to be reserved for the older members of the Senior School. Scripture examination day was however a highlight, as after register in the morning, a visiting examiner came and asked a few questions of the class in general, which were answered by the more intelligent members. The visitor then went into the next room and your class was free to go home for the rest of the day. At Christmas-time and on special occasions, if we were very good, Miss Roland, the Headmistress, gave us a great treat; we were allowed to watch the antics of a puppet on a stick which danced up and down on a board. I think I only saw this gentleman two or three times. I think some tribute should be paid to Miss Burnell's efforts with the top members of the school. I wonder if she has any idea of the number of scholarship pupils which have passed through her hands.

Reflections From Mr. J. Bradshaw 1926 - 1931:

To be set another composition by Miss Burnell after nearly three decades was quite a shock, and what a subject - 'I remember'. Recollection of junior school life after so long is like looking into a kaleidoscope, the pieces suddenly fell together to make up a picture. One early fragment is when I was put into the wrong classroom during the first couple of days at school by a well-meaning cousin - I screamed the place down. Another was when I was summoned to a more senior classroom to be told what a naughty girl my elder sister had been and given a note for our parents informing them of this. I regret to say that this was put down a nearby convenient drain. The buildings seem to have been disturbed very little over the years; Mountain Ash is still there but not quite so impressive as it was, though it has now been augmented by some very pleasant flowering trees. The horse trough that used to freeze over in the winter and cause much speculation as to whether it would bear our weight, has gone from near the Boys' entrance. Miss Rowland's dais with the judicial desk from which she used to entertain the very young ones by playing 'Fly away Peter, fly away Paul', with the aid of little pieces of red paper, has been moved to the other side of the hall, but to compensate for these differences Miss Burnell is still there. The most displeasing alteration for me took place when they deprived the old school of its proud and honourable name of 'Merrywood'. I regret that very much.

Mrs. E.E. Brewer:

I was Edna Matthews and I started at this school in 1920. Miss Wilkins was my teacher in the first class. I have forgotten the teachers in between but I remember Miss Gay in Standard 1, Miss Burnell in Standard 2 and Miss Kirklands in the top class. Miss Rowlands was our Headmistress and we all loved her very much. The highlight of the day for me and for many of my friends was after open service in the hall, when she would gently lift a wooden puppet out of her desk. It was jointed and had coloured ribbons on it and she would make it dance for us in time with music, played on the piano. I look back to many happy days spent at the school and am very pleased to think that my two boys had the opportunity to begin their school life at the same school.

From Mr. & Mrs. Sayer (Sill & Joan):

It is now some thirty years since we had our early schooling at Merrywood Junior School - the name Southville Primary, a comparatively recent title, hold no memories for us. Thinking back to those days, it is personalities rather than activities one recalls most easily. The members of the staff we remember were Miss Rowland, Headmistress, the Misses Burnell, Gay, Llewellyn, Beer, Pinkerton, Gliddon, Edgar, Kirkland and Wilkins. We remember a happy school where every member of staff gave cheerfully of their best to lay a good foundation for more advanced schooling. Miss Rowland, 'Connie' behind her back, was considered a bit of a tartar by the pupils and, we suspect, by the staff. On reflection however, she was a first-class headmistress who did a wonderful job of work. She had a passionate desire to hear pupils speaking correctly. Many, besides ourselves, must remember standing on her chair after prayers, carefully reciting the names of the days of the week and the months of the year. Other memories? Anglo-French week in the early 30s when the boys and girls learned Maypole dancing and joined schools from all over Bristol in a display, wonderful Christmas parties with every classroom decorated, the Sand Tray with realistic desert scenes. These are but a few of the happy memories which come readily to mind. Looking back over the years we realise what an excellent start in life we were given.

From Mrs. M. Mulligan - Memories of Southville School:

My earliest recollection of 'Merrywood' as it was called in my day, was dancing round the Maypole, the girls in white dresses and the boys in white shirts and grey trousers, to an audience of parents and friends. I can also remember learning tables, the whole class singing them together at the top of their voices. Another day I shall not forget was the one when all children had to be vaccinated because of a smallpox scare. The mere thought of the needle made several children faint. Miss Rowland, the Headmistress, was very stern and everyone lived in terror of being sent to her. Miss Gay, Miss Gliddon, and Miss Kirkland were teachers and Miss Burnell, who is still at 'Southville' carrying on the tradition of the school. The Christmas fancy dress parties were thoroughly enjoyed, the costumes mostly made with crepe paper. On Friday afternoons children were allowed to take their own story books or toys to school, so Friday became a day to look forward to. But most of I still remember the happiness which I always felt in my school days - I cannot think of one day when I did not want to go. I feel sure that my son also will always carry happy memories of Southville.

A class in Merrywood Infants School, believed to have been taken in 1909.

From Mr. H.E. Lewis:

Memories of personalities will, I am sure, always remain with me. I well remember Miss Rowland, the Head Mistress, so insistent that silence must prevail at all times in the hall, and Miss Kirkland, so strict and completely in command. Then of course, one always had a favourite teacher. My choice was Miss Gay who was so quiet and understanding. These were, to me, happy days.

Mr. R.E. Gale. School Reminiscences:

Since my school days, which covered the period of the 'Thirties', Southville appears to have changed its face in some ways. My earliest recollections are happy ones when in Merrywood Junior School, as it was then called. I acquired my basic training under the eagle eyes of a Miss Knowles, and later Miss Burnell for whom I had a deep respect (a look from the latter was enough to command it!). It is difficult to recall clearly the routine work, but for me the morning service, with news items and P.T. sessions, held pride of place (no doubt due to the amount of mental exertion required!). A fundamental difference in approach to the modern pupil will be apparent when I tell of the occasion when I was placed between two girls to shame me and had my left hand tied behind my back in order to teach me to write with my right hand. (The girls asked for a transfer!). 'Merrywood' changed its name to 'Southville' I believe, in 1936.

From Mr. R.E.R. Edmonds:

Twenty-five years ago, Merrywood School, as it was then known, was quite a 'power in the land' in all aspects of its activities. The teachers, although having to deal with some extremely varied types of pupil, achieved a very good 'finished product' and I personally have to thank them for the basis of my future. In spite of hard work in the classroom, sport was not neglected and Merrywood School was one of the foremost names in most branches, particularly football and swimming. I have always lived in the vicinity of the school and it is refreshing to see the boys and girls carrying on the traditions. I still follow very closely the reports in the newspapers concerning the soccer teams and am very pleased to learn that several Southville boys have been selected during the past season to represent Bristol Boys.

From Enid Comstock (nee Tanner):

I must have been very eager to start school at Merrywood, as one of my earliest memories is of the day I wandered away from home to join my older sister, Mary Tanner, in the first class, where my frantic mother found me calmly absorbing the reading lesson led, I believe, by Miss Wilkins. The day came though, when I could join the other children after play-time and march two and two around the big hall, trying our best to keep in step with the piano. It must be the little things that children remember - those icy bottles of milk in the winter. A large glass jar of gummy horse-chestnut buds unfolding in the spring sun; the painting in the hall of Sir Walter Raleigh telling sea stories to two young boys; the 'hospital' smell as we lined up for inoculations and the pleasantly mixed aroma of coffee and tea coming from the teachers' lounge. (I do not think so! E.M.B.) Then there was the time we danced the Maypole - was it at Clifton High? The boys in grey shorts and the girls in yellow and white checked dresses, which the mothers had made. Donald Carlisle was my partner and we got rather muddled, but our proud parents and teachers told us we had all done beautifully. And the day we received the Coronation mugs filled with chocolates - mine were almost gone by the time I got home to lunch! We must have learnt 'reading, 'riting and 'rithmetic' somewhere during those years but it must have been a very painless experience. There came a morning when Miss Jones sent us off to the scholarship examinations with such confidence, for she knew we were going to pass - and pass we did!

Here is part of an interview given in 1987 by Mrs Elsie Everitt, who was an early pupil at Merrywood Infants. The remainder of her story comes under the St Paul's School heading.

Mrs. Elsie Everitt, interviewed by Bernice Conway - 6.2.1987:

I was a pupil at Merrywood Road School. I started there on the day it opened in 1908. We did not do any work on the first day. There were lots of visitors and the school was opened officially. The Headmistress's name was Miss Rowland. I remember that the floor of the classroom was tiered, each row higher than the one the front. That way the teacher could keep an eye on all the children. When you were old enough to go to the Senior School in Howard Road, a Mr. Dowling came from that school to see if your work was good enough. He looked at my books for a long time and could not seem to make up his mind. He walked away, then came back again, had another look and finally said "All right". If my work had not been good enough, I would have had to stay on longer at Merrywood Road School.

I didn't like it in the Senior School. They were very fond of using the cane. I was in Miss Kelly's class. She beat me one day with the edge of a ruler. I had deep weals across my hands. My mother complained to the school and decided to move me. At the Merrywood Schools a New Testament was given to each child, who excelled in religious knowledge by The Religious Tract society and Mary Procter, in memory of her husband. Miss K. Wood received one in 1915. Mrs. Procter was the widow of Alderman Procter, who had put in the 'Boulevard of Trees' along The Cut on Coronation Road in 1873.

At the Beauley Road schools in 1913 the price of a school dinner was 4d. This was for a meal consisting of meat, vegetables and dessert. Despite this low cost for a meal, times were hard and in 1914 the Headmaster had difficulty in getting coal for the school furnaces, the consequences of this being that many of the pupils and staff were absent because of the severe cold. Later the staff thought that they received a bad deal when they were refused permission to install a wireless aerial in the staff room and later in 1925 the Headmaster had cause for complaint when he was refused permission to install a telephone. When he wanted to make a phone call, he had to use a public call box or use the phone of an obliging tradesman. Eight years later this Headmaster was still complaining about the lack of a telephone. In April 1937 Merrywood Secondary School was transferred to Downton Road, Knowle and the site became two schools, Southville Senior Boys and Southville Girls schools.

1937	Beauley Road became two single sex schools Southville Senior Boys and Southville Senior Girls.
1941	The Southville Schools took pupils from South Street Girls, Luckwell Girls, Luckwell Boys, Windmill Hill and Ashton Gate Boys, when their schools were damaged or destroyed by bombs.
1944	The Southville Schools became Secondary Modern Schools for pupils who failed the '11 Plus'
1947	Leaving age raised to fifteen.
1962	Girls and Boys Schools combined to form Southville Secondary Mixed School.
1967	Pupils from Marksbury Road transferred to Southville. Miss Uppington became the Headmistress.
1971	Southville amalgamated with Ashton Park Secondary School and became the Lower School.
1984	Ashton Park Lower School closed on 20th July.

In the early 20s the Bristol Education Committee Housewifery Centre used the house at No. 96 Beauley Road for classes. Here cookery, needlework and house management courses were taught to Merrywood Senior Girls of the Beauley Road School, across the road. Midwifery classes were taught by Miss Thompson and Miss Blade. Certificates were given to those girls who successfully completed the courses.

St. Paul's Church School.

On December 28th 1870, a meeting was held at St. Paul's Vicarage where it was proposed that a committee be appointed to carry out the erection of schools in the parish of St. Paul's. It was also decided that Sir Greville Smythe be applied to for land to build on. On January 21st 1871, Mr J Neale, Architect, was approached to supply plans, not exceeding £1,200, and on February 25th, it was agreed that his plans be accepted. Action was quickly taken and the school was completed by August 26th 1872. Thomas Josiah Wright was appointed as headmaster. He died, aged seventy-nine in 1924 and is buried at St. Paul's Church. In July 1877, the decision was taken to accept a tender of £648 to build an Infant School attached to the main school. This was completed by the end of 1877 with Miss Alicia Howell taking the post of Headmistress. When the school closed in 1959, it had only eighty pupils. The building was demolished and the site bought by Holy Cross Church.

As with all schools, some liked St. Paul's and some did not.

We continue with the interview of Mrs. Everitt, who liked the school.

I was at St. Paul's School, Dean Lane from 1912 till 1914. I liked it very much. The Headmistress was Miss Stevens. I also remember the teachers Mrs Breadmere, Miss Johnson and Miss Stone. Mrs. Breadmere taught Standards 6, 7 and X7, all in one room. X7 were girls who had reached standard 7 but were not yet fourteen years old, so they stayed at school to learn additional things, like how to use a sewing machine. Boys and girls were taught separately. Girls upstairs and boys down. Mr Deacon was Headmaster of the boys section. He was very popular with the boys and they all liked and respected him. Infants were taught in the back part of the school. The caretaker's name was Mr. Fox. On Saints Days we went for a service at St. Paul's then had the rest of the day off. On Empire Day we gathered in the front playground to sing patriotic songs such as 'Flag of Britain'. All the girls wore red, white and blue ribbons on our pinnys. Good Friday we went to church and then walked in pairs to the Vicarage in Acraman's Road. We sang to Canon Griffiths and church dignitaries. Afterwards we sat on the vicarage lawn and were given buns to eat.

Some pupils at Dean Lane School did not learn very much. Discipline was often severe. One student of the 1920s recalled:-
'Mr. Manning, an ex-army man, flogged the boys enthusiastically. Professor Deacon, who was renowned for teaching his own system of shorthand, was also very strict. He rode a motorcycle, an FN, with a huge block engine, which sounded like a train. He sat up there all proud and no matter the weather, his hat never fell off. Deacon would give Mrs. Beardmore a lift home and they would shoot off withthis tremendous roar'. There were lots of fights with boys from Holy Cross. The main children's playground was the old trolley line which ran between Catherine Mead Street and Essex Street. Before the swimming baths were built, we played football on small fields at the back. Because of the many schools in the area, by 1915 street fighting had become a regular after-school event. Fierce battles

between Beauley Road (so called 'Upper Class') and Dean Lane ('Lower Class') institutions were frequent. Although no-one would give details in later years, a boy was seriously injured. On Stackpool Road in the 1920s, running battles took place between Merrywood Senior and Dean Lane School. Schools on Dean Lane were very close together, only separated by a thin fence, so fighting also went on there at playtime and after school. Yet children played together happily after a general free for all.

Holy Cross School

The first Southville Catholic School was opened at the back of East Street in 1857 by Arthur Hawkins Ward, Warden of St. Raphael's. He lived in Southville Road. With sound backing from the district, Ward established this small school in conjunction with a church. By 1874 the school had grown so large that it had to move to Redcliffe. Thirty-seven years were to pass before building began on a school in Dean Lane in 1911. The Holy Cross new schools opened on July 4th 1912. The sum of £3,000 still had to be raised. Entertainments, concerts, a café, skittle alley and sale of work were put on in October 1912 at the schools in Dean Lane, to raise money to pay off the debt. 'An old parishioner', of the original Bedminster Holy Cross, unnamed in a manuscript provided by Father Healey, wrote this about the old school and the new one of 1912.

Holy Cross schools. The laying of the foundation stone on September 16th, 1911.
The school was opened in 1912 and the church in 1922.

We had a school attached to the Church. This was a mixed school and at the time of which I am speaking, (the early 1870s) was taught by Sisters from the 'Blue Nuns' Convent in Clifton Wood, now removed to Rodney Place, Clifton Down Road, and it is an interesting coincidence that the Holy Cross Schools returned again to Bedminster, after the lapse of more than a generation. And so now, after thirty-seven years, we are about to make another new departure and retrace our steps once more to dear old Bedminster, but what a changed Bedminster do we return, as compared with the one we left! The growth of the district has been phenomenal, and there are now many hundreds of modern houses, well suited to the requirements of such a congregation as ours, within easy distance of the new Schools, Presbytery and proposed Church, and we can reasonably hope to see an increasing Catholic population gradually spring up around our church and schools, and I trust, one equally loyal and united as was that which once formed the congregation of the original Holy Cross Church.

John Bevin, Licentiate R.I.B.A., Architect, Bristol, wrote this about the new schools of Dean Lane:-

The Schools have been designed to afford accommodation for 350 children, viz. 200 boys and girls, and 150 Infants. The building contains two storeys, the Ground Floor for Infants, which contains three classrooms, marching room, cloakroom, teachers' room and lavatory, and wide corridor. The Upper Floor is for boys and girls, and is approached by fireproof staircases, and contains four classrooms, teachers room, cloakroom and lavatory, - also a wide corridor. Each classroom accommodates 50 children and is left-hand lighted. Size of rooms:- 25ft x 20 ft. Many of these rooms are divided by moveable glazed screens. The Schools are so planned as to obtain the maximum amount of sunshine, while cross ventilation is provided in all cases. The materials used in the treatment of the exterior, are red facing bricks in bands, pilasters and string courses, freestone dressings, rubber brick arches and cement rough-casting to face of walls down to the brick plinth; roof covered with Bridgwater tiling. The interior treatment is simple and well lighted. The floors are of fireproof construction, covered with pitch-pine bricks. All walls have a dado of glazed tiles. The building is warmed by means of a low pressure hot water system, and well ventilated. Large playgrounds are provided. The Schools are designed in the Georgian style; the aim of the Architect has been to combine utility with dignity.

By the late 1920s many Southville Roads had a private school. One of the best known was Miss A. Berryman's school. This began in Acramans Road and moved in 1936 to 109 Coronation Road.

Working people wanted further education to keep up with the growth of industry, union membership and more importantly, the increased knowledge of their children. Local churches had organised night classes since the 1870s and Southville people eagerly sought after knowledge. The co-op movement in Southville at Dean Street and Raleigh Road encouraged night schooling. Young people responded enthusiastically, particularly as night school became an accepted way of dating their partners. This community growth continued until interrupted by World War 2.

MEDICAL MATTERS

Medicine

It is a tribute to the robust constitutions of early Southville residents that so many lived to advanced age. For, as the new district merged with Bedminster, the contagious diseases of the age spread.

Hannah Snow of Coronation Road died in 1864 at the age of one hundred years. John Hare and Jos. Cottle lived to see their eighties. A later minister, Revd. George Wood, did not retire until he was seventy one and died in 1902 aged eighty eight. These people had lived through the scourges of the time - typhoid and cholera. But there are also many gravestones and records of the early and mid 1800s showing it was an acceptable fact of that time that many young people would die. Women lost their lives in childbirth, or the complications of it. 'Wasting diseases' were another form of early death. The wealthy were attended by doctors at Redcliffe and from Clifton. Southville did not become a popular area for the medical profession until the General Hospital had become established, yet the district was concerned with health matters from early times.

Following Jenner's development of vaccination against smallpox in 1798, a Bedminster clinic at Malago was set up in 1803 to administer the 'cowpox' shots. A few years later a voluntary clinic was established in Dean Lane close to North Street. Although no official records exist, we have dug into local research for reference. Ashmead's Map (dated 1826) shows a row of buildings along Dean Lane - opposite to where the Bristol South Baths would later be built. This is where the old clinic once existed. It was close to many apothecaries, midwives and early Bedminster doctors.

More than a century later the dreaded 'fever clinic', which many older Southville residents recall shudderingly from childhood, would be in the same area. Workers on the New Cut and from nearby mining pits were able to receive minor medical treatment at this clinic. Miners had surgeons at the pits, and the Cut workers had medical officers on duty along the new river road.

All too often injuries were received by workers from over-indulgence in drink and from fighting - especially at the nearby 'Star Inn'. Until Southville physicians became established, apothecaries reigned supreme. Poorer people were dependent upon them, since remedies could be bought at a reasonable price and almost anything was sold over the counter. Arsenic and strychnine would be purchased for tonics, brimstone and treacle for cooling the blood. Leeches were popular for putting on septic wounds to suck out the poison. Local women made a living by seeking out leeches in the Malago and other local marshes and streams to sell to apothecaries and to the 'medicine women'. Poppy heads were popular purchases at apothecary shops, for these kept both sick children and old folk quiet. In fact, opium was still readily available in much later years. Medicines compounded in the back of dispensaries of local apothecaries were kept well hidden from the eyes of the public and the whole operation became surrounded with mystique.

'White witches' gathered herbs and common weeds from the hedgerows and brooks of Southville. They were 'good' witches and were renowned in early Southville for helping to cure sick animals and for producing spells for dry cows and barren animals. Where small farms proliferated on the Southville side of North Street, 'white witches' were active for many years, perhaps until the turn of the 20th century.

Women played an important role in the health care of our district. They were essential for the all too frequent 'lying-ins' and equally common 'laying-out'. Male midwives were not uncommon but most mothers preferred to be tended by a local woman, skilled by years of experience. Perhaps also women midwives were more sympathetic. Until the 1920s, most babies were born at home. 'Medicine women' tended to colic, coughs, broken bones and various common ills - they even pulled teeth. As well as collecting common household items such as spider's webs to help stop bleeding, these women depended on apothecaries for their remedies. J Mather and G Beke were among the earliest apothecaries in Bedminster and these men did a flourishing business. Even with the help of apothecaries and home nurses, the death toll of Bedminster, and therefore Southville, continued to be high.

The funeral business was brisk. Carpenters, stablers and even accountants engaged in this occupation as a side line.

THE CITY FUNERAL MART (1820 Advertisement)

First class funerals	=	Five pounds
Second class	=	Four pounds
Third class	=	Three pounds
Fourth class	=	Two pounds ten shillings
Fifth class	=	One pound fifteen shillings

All include cloaks and hat bands. Children's funerals cost ten shillings.

A funeral procession in Dartmoor Street. The final journey accomplished in some style.

With the establishment of the General Hospital on the other side of The Cut, hopes of medical help were raised. The hospital opened November 1st 1832. There were only ten beds.

A cholera epidemic broke out in 1832, affecting not only the poor of Bedminster but the affluent residents of Coronation Road and adjacent roads. The General Hospital was used as a cholera hospital and local people, schooled in nursing and medicine, rallied to help. Five hundred and sixty four people died from the disease. Another epidemic broke out in 1849 when four hundred and forty four people lost their lives. By 1848 a local Board of Health was set up in the district to see that the health of residents was being safeguarded. This Health Board was given added muscle by the introduction of the Sanitary Committee of 1851. Dr David Davis the Chief of the Board swept through Southville with dire warnings for unsanitary slaughter houses and scavenger tips, to clean up or face prosecution. Scavenger yards in Dean Lane and Greenway Bush Lane were fined after failing to clean up and many 'public nuisances' had been cleaned up by 1860.

In 1850 a Registrar for Births and Deaths was established at 26 Dean Street and John Carter became the first official. By getting local people to register births of children, care could be taken to attempt to secure their survival. And to add clout to this law, a charge of 7/6d was made if the birth of a child was not registered before 42 days had elapsed.

Efforts to improve care and survival were impeded by lack of sewerage facilities in Southville. Earth closets were the commonest form of sanitation and even when St Paul's School was built in 1870 it was provided with these conveniences. Such closets were emptied at night by workers desperate for employment. Ashes were used for disinfectant. In 1872 earth closets were being advertised in local newspapers at a cost of £4 4s for adult sizes and £2 15s for child sizes. The earth for use in such facilities was delivered free. It was not until 1875 that sewers were dug in the more prosperous parts of Southville.

The poorer residents of Southville who lived in courts or 'paddocks' off Dean Lane and at the back of East Street, had to endure cess pits and often open ground holes. This state of affairs continued until the turn of the 20th century. The energetic work of local health officials did have great impact. There were only twenty-nine deaths from the cholera epidemic of 1866 and the disease began a slow eclipse. Yet cholera still claimed lives in the 20th century.

In 1840 Dr Thomas Tovey Smart became the Medical Officer for the Parish of Bedminster and thus Southville. He was only 26 years of age. For this important position he was paid £900 per annum. Dr Smart became Southville's most influential doctor and within ten years had established his own practice on Southville Road, at Mona Lodge. He was named Public Vaccinator of Southville in 1867 and Medical Officer of the Bedminster Union. He died in August 1882 aged 68 years. Dr Smart's successful practice together with the General Hospital's growth and the cleansing of Southville, lead to many more medical men coming to the area. Early doctors dressed grandly, sporting coat tails, top hats and elaborately decorated shirts. Gold watch chains and fobs, together with expensively topped canes or sticks, enhanced the effect. One later Southville physician, Dr William Napper Neville of Acraman's Road (1903), had earlier had a practice in West Street. From there he visited important patients in Southville in an ornate carriage with his team of Dalmatians running behind. We do not know if these Dalmatians came with him to Southville.

As with apothecaries before them, chemists moved swiftly and powerfully into Southville. In 1870 John Durant established the Capsule Factory in Murray Street off Catherine Mead Street. He lived in Myrtle House on Dean Lane but later moved to Southville Road and by 1903 his family were living in Acramans Road.

By 1875 other chemists were trading in Dean Lane and by the early 1890s several chemists were opening at the Dean Lane end of North Street. Another chemist, James Allen is listed in 1893 at 10 Peartree Terrace, a line of shops just by Merrywood Road in North Street. In 1902 a Mr. Dunford took over this chemist business. Unhappily he killed himself by taking poison in 1939 and Hedley Price bought the shop, so owning two chemists shops in North Street. Until the 1940s anything and everything was sold over the counter and the most curious oils, ointments and tonics were widely advertised. Women were not employed in the chemist's mysterious dispensaries until much later. By the mid 1870s members of the medical profession were growing in Coronation and Stackpool Roads. In 1872 Dr Keall was at 'Nelson Lodge' in Coronation Road. This house remained a doctor's residence until recent years. The 1880s saw Dr Sidney Gent at 60 Coronation Road but in 1886 he had moved to Southville Place with the naturist, Sidney Hutton. Dr William FitzWilliam Carter was at 48 and 49 Coronation Road and by 1900 was joined by Doctors John Thompson and Wallace. Dr Henry Cook was the first medical man to move into No1 Dean Lane (Linthorpe House). This house was built in 1881 by William Kingston as a gentlemen's house. After Dr Cook had made it into a surgery, it remained as such until the present day. Cook had previously practised on Stackpool Road. He was joined by Dr Fred Logan in 1889 and both doctors stayed until the 1920s.

A 19th century photograph of John Durant's capsule factory in Murray Road.

Dentists

Whilst dentistry was largely a DIY matter for poorer people, dentists were established in Southville in 1850. Surgeons E Clark & Sons operated near the 'Hen & Chicken', perhaps helped on by some strong draughts beforehand! While 'laughing gas' was a fairly early invention, anaesthesia was not generally available at dentists and thus visits to dental surgeons were postponed until absolutely vital. Dr T Freestone, a dental and general surgeon, operated from Coronation Road from the early 1870s. Later he moved between Zion Church and the Grosvenor Public House, perhaps to drown the howling. In later years - from the 1920s until the 1950s - the most dreaded Southville dentist, who operated from Freestone's earlier practice, was Dr Boyd Joll. His apprentices would pull a tooth on Saturday mornings for sixpence. Dr Joll is said to have made his own 'laughing gas' but older Southville people testify that only the doctor did any laughing. He was very well known figure in Southville and was called names we are unable to print. Even the police fled at the sight of him!

Nurses and Midwives

A Mrs. Lewis who resided in Alpha Road was a monthly nurse in the 1870s. Nurse Forder, also of Alpha Road was a parish nurse for St Paul's in the early 1880s. She was helped by many female visitors to the sick.
1900 Miss Watts, 103 Greenway Bush Lane, District Nurse.
1903 Mrs Harriet Amundsen, 2 Florence Place. Nurse Hayes, Southville Place, Midwife.
1910 Miss Eva Bird, 40 Southville Place, Midwife.
1919 Mrs Matilda Ann Midgley, 9 Merrywood Road. Mrs Florence England, 17 Kingston Road.
1920s Mrs Emily Westlake, 68 Raleigh Road. (She delivered Russ Conway) Mrs Smith (she wore black boots and black stockings and was reputed as being a 'battle axe'!)
1925 Mrs Mary Ann Latcham, 14 Alpha Road, Midwife.

The 'Black Hole' mentioned often by people interviewed, operated in Dean Lane opposite the Swimming Baths in the 1920s and 1930s. The sinister looking building had blacked out windows and local mothers hurried their children past telling them not to look - so naturally they did. Children treated there had their heads deloused and gentian violet put on sores. Those vaccinated had to wear red arm bands so that others would not knock against them. Children were taken back and forth in a black van, rather like a 'Black Maria'. This van, called the 'Fever Van' was often driven by Mr Horner of Howard Road. The 'Black Hole'
closed in 1936.

We end this brief account of medicine in Southville by acknowledging that many medical men and women have been omitted because of lack and space.

POLICE, LAW AND ORDER

From 1759 each parish in the county had a chief constable and 100 petty constables. Joseph Williams was the Chief Constable of Bedminster at this time with one hundred men between the ages of 18 and 30.

The formation of the constabulary arose because of the war with France and Pitt's subsequent Militia Bill of 1759. The Militia and the constabulary, although formed at the same time, had entirely separate duties. The Somerset Militia consisted of officers and eight hundred and forty other ranks and in 1761 the Militia was quartered at Bedminster. The early association of the constabulary and Militia appears to have quietly disintegrated, for by 1797 the 'Bristol Volunteers' was formed with William Gore as the Lieutenant Colonel.

The primary power in Bristol was, however, held by the Sheriff. Since 1373 Bristol had its own Assizes and from 1499 the Mayor and Aldermen were automatically JPs. This system sometimes led to abuses. This is how the Reverend Emmanuel Collins came to be dispensing justice and marrying people at the Star in the 1740s. The Star at the time was the main court for Bedminster, including Southville. Informers as well as good citizens brought offenders before the Magistrates Court. No doubt this system accounted for many of the area's early street battles.

The Sheriff's men held the following ranks - Yeomen, Sergeants and Constables. The sergeants were splendidly attired in blue coats, red waistcoats and black velvet breeches. Sam Baber, of Ashton Cottage, North Street, was an early Sheriff's man and fellow officer with Sir Hugh Smythe. He is mentioned in one book as Sir Hugh's 'Strong Arm' in the 1780s. Samuel's son Harry Baber was born in 1787. Harry was also a Sheriff. He lived in various places in Southville and in 1850 lived in Southville Buildings, Coronation Road, with his wife Mary. Baber was another of the influential citizens who attended the opening of St Paul's church. As well as being a Sheriff, Harry Baber was also an Auctioneer. This was then a powerful position. In 1846 he had been given a political sinecure in the Council Office. Baber was the leading figure of the law in Southville.

As early as 1740 there were Water Bailiffs on the River Avon so that by 1809 there were River Police patrolling The Cut. The Bedminster and early Southville area was mainly patrolled by night watchmen or 'Charlies'. Generally these were positions given to former council employees. In 1774 Bristol employed one hundred and fifty watchmen who were paid to patrol eight hours in winter and seven hours in summer. Wearing their large cloaks and hats, the watchmen frequently dozed away their working nights. However, since the local 'Charlies' were well known by Bedminster and Southville people, they were often called upon to intercede in some local crimes.

With the opening of churches in Southville in 1830 the Beadles and Church leaders exercised some power in the new community, so until 1831 law and order was controlled by Petty Constables, the Militia, Sheriffs, Yeomen, Sergeants, Water Bailiffs, Night Watchmen and Churchmen. However, within the year all this broke down with the advent of the Reform riots.

The riots started with the consecration of St Paul's Church, Southville on the 24th October 1831 by the Bishop of Bath and Wells. He had to be protected from angry local people and drove off followed by a volley of stones. It became a full blooded riot on the night of 29th/30th October with the burning of the Mansion House, most of Queen Square and the new Gaol on the Cut which had only been opened eleven years before, at a cost of £60,000.

The mob that marched on the Gaol was well armed with bludgeons, hatchets and iron palisades. They also had sledgehammers and with these they smashed a hole in the prison gates. A man crawled through, drew the bolts and some three hundred rioters poured in. One hundred and seventy prisoners were released; the prison Governor's house was ransacked and everything moveable thrown into The Cut and as the tide was on the ebb, it was all swept away. The house was set on fire along with the Chapel, the Treadmill and the Gallows.

All this was watched by thousands of people along Coronation Road. These included law enforcement officers who were powerless to stop the destruction. Eventually, with the help of the Militia, the rioters were contained and one hundred and twenty seven arrests were made. Charges against twenty-five were dropped and eighty-one of the remaining one hundred and two were found guilty. They were given sentences ranging from imprisonment to transportation for life. Five were sentenced to death. They were Christopher Davies, William Clarke, Thomas Gregory, Joseph Kayes and Richard Vines. The last named was a mentally handicapped person and had his sentence reduced to transportation for life. The remaining four men were hanged from the battered entrance (which still stands) of the new Gaol at midday on 27th January 1832, in front of a large crowd along Coronation Road.

An early photograph of the Old Gaol most likely taken from the tower of St. Paul's church. Only the gatehouse of this once extensive building now remains. The sloping pathways in the foreground led to the Gaol Ferry, out of sight to the left of the photograph.

Following the riots, the Municipal Corporation Act of 1835 provided local police forces. The Bedminster Police Force which covered Southville was headed by Inspector Bosworth. Ironically, while waiting for the Police Station to be completed, the Police rented office space from Samuel Clarke, whose nephew had been hanged at the Gaol for his part in the riots. Clarke's premises were on the corner of Charlotte Street and provided easy access to the growing Police Station. The Police paid Clarke seven shillings per week.

A trial was held at The Star in 1821 of John Harwood who had thrown a stone at his girl friend and killed her. The presiding magistrate was Thomas Hassell. He was one of the men who petitioned for St Paul's to be built in Southville. Harwood was found guilty and hanged at the new Gaol. This was the first hanging there. Harwood's body was skinned and the skin was made into a book-cover! Because Hassell was by trade a skinner and tanner and well known as a severe magistrate, it has always been thought in Southville that Hassell arranged the gruesome act. However no written proof exists to substantiate this. Hassell lived at Bedminster House from 1805 until it became Bedminster Academy and members of his family later inter-married with several well-known Southville families.

Sarah Harriet Thomas, an eighteen year old servant, was hanged publicly at the new Gaol in April 1849. Local churchmen had petitioned the government and the defence of Sarah was particularly vigorous from William Day Wills who represented Zion church. The execution was watched by thousands of Southville people who had queued since dawn to see the spectacle. This was the last public hanging of a woman in Britain.

The righteous of Southville had pressed for the new Gaol to be built on the opposite side of The Cut as they did not particularly want it on their side. The imposing new Gaol opened in 1820 as houses were being constructed on Coronation road. The prison represented authority and, in particular, emphasised the authority of Southville magistrates. The new Gaol was closed in 1883 and later demolished, apart from the gateway.

The original Bedminster Police Station was opened in 1836 on the site of the present derelict building in East Street. This building was pulled down and replaced by the present castellated police/fire station in 1882. Much of the early police work dealt in assaults and fights in the Bedminster beer houses. Police Constables were often assaulted. But for the most part the officers were known and respected in the community. Theft and burglary were major problems in law enforcement, but because the punishment was so severe, few people were prosecuted.

The Reverend Israel Lewis of Long Ashton called on Inspector Bosworth for help in curbing disturbances between railwaymen and navigators (navvies) in November 1838. It took the Inspector and ten Police Constables to bring back the trouble makers. In 1840 John Smith was charged with assaulting several officers in Queen Street (Southville). He was charged and fined one and sixpence.

Some of the well known policemen of the area were: George Yates of the Lamb Inn, West

A view at the turn of the 20th century of East Street from the Bedminster Bridge end. The fortress-like Police Station is to the right and an electric tram can just be recognised in the centre of the road.

Street. He was the first constable of Bedminster. John Smele of 1 Ashton Terrace, Coronation Road, a Southville Landowner, was a Police Constable in 1848.

Inspector Black, the great, great grandfather of local boy Reg Nott, lived in one of the early police houses on Charlotte Street.

Inspector J A Gardner, Sgt Simms and policemen Manning, Hamilton and Warren were early police officers in Bedminster. Many lived in police houses in Charlotte Street, although this did not deter the many brawls in the beer-houses close-by.

Another Southville resident who became a Police Constable in1856 was Israel Maynard. In St Paul's churchyard is the grave of John Baker who was born in 1827 and died 25th July 1889 aged sixty-two. He was a member of Bedminster Police Force for twenty years.

Supt. J H Harris lived in Southville Road. He ran Bedminster Police Station.

Inspector John Davies lived on Langton Crescent, Merrywood Lane in 1886. After he retired he moved to 28, Howard Road and acted as a coal agent. Davies was on the Bedminster Board of Guardians and ran for this office again in 1898.

In 1886 Frederick Howell a police officer lived at York House, Milford Street. He was related to Charles Howell, who at the time lived at Merrywood Villa.

Later policemen also acted as firemen. William Frampton, who lived in Charlotte Street in 1890, acted in both capacities.

Inspector May lived in Greville Road in the 1880s and 1890s. May, tall and commanding, was an imposing figure in his splendid brass-clad uniform as he walked from Greville Road to Bedminster Police Station.

Southville people in the 1920s do not always remember policemen as kindly folk. The police escorted mothers and babies across roads and smiled at little girls, but older men of today remember being harshly treated as boys, sometimes hit with a policeman's night stick or the flick of a heavy cape on their tender ears.

Later law.

Records of this time are concerned with petty crime, larceny and brawling. Accidents of the period were mostly from gas poisoning, also, since the railings along The Cut were incomplete, people of all ages were still falling into it. Most offences were for street betting, passing or hiding slips. Venturing 'a bob or two' on racing was very common, but it was still illegal. The Bedminster police usually ignored both 'running' and betting shops, for some of them placed bets themselves. They only cracked down when it became too open. Generally betting was not in any way considered a crime by the local people.

Quarter Sessions Reports

A report from the Quarter Sessions dated 7th April 1832 states that James Underhill and David Griffiths, two youths of sixteen years of age, were placed at the bar charged with robbing Mr. John Hare and others of a variety of articles including a decanter and candlestick. It appeared that the articles were left safe within Zion Chapel at Bedminster Bridge, of which the prosecutors were the Trustees and that on the morning of 27th February some thieves entered the Chapel and stole them. The prisoners were seen in suspicious circumstances near the Chapel by the Watchman. They were seen to get over a wall and enter a garden at the back of the Chapel, a ladder was placed against a wall. The prisoners were seen by the patrol and Underhill was captured as he ran away. A chisel was found on one of the prisoners which fitted the marks on the door that they had broken open. They were both found guilty. Griffiths was sentenced to one year's imprisonment and Underhill to seven years transportation.

Another report dated 12th February 1898 states that John Morgan, aged nineteen years had been charged with stealing a duck valued at three shillings, the property of Virtue Bray of 20 Kingston Road, Southville. Selina Jackson saw Morgan take the duck from the yard of the Dean Lane Colliery, and P C Gibbs stated that he found it at No. 11 Dean Lane where the accused lived. Edith Mary Bray, daughter of the prosecutor identified the bird and said that their backyard abutted onto the Colliery yard. The accused vowed that he picked up the duck from beneath some timber. He was sentenced to a month's imprisonment.

Taken from Police Occurrence Book - Bristol Record Office

3rd March 1837
About one o'clock on Thursday morning of the 2nd instant, PC 193 - Moore, when on duty,

was going along Dean Lane, Bedminster, observed two women coming towards him and suspecting that all was not correct, he stopped one of them for a few moments. After a while a man named Holder came up and stated that the one stopped had robbed him of nearly £5. The policeman left the one he had detained with Holder and pursued the other, whom he soon overtook, endeavouring to secrete a handkerchief in a doorway. On taking her into custody, he distinctly saw her drop a small parcel which he found contained £2 3s 6d. He returned to Holder and took them both to the police station at Bedminster. They were searched and nearly the whole amount was found on their persons. On Friday they were taken before the Magistrates, but discharged, in consequence of Holder refusing to prosecute.

28th February 1838
A male waiter - Robert Beany, whilst in a state of intoxication, fell out of the garret window of 'The Star' public house, Bedminster, and broke one of his legs. He was taken on a stretcher to the Guinea Street Hospital where immediate attention was paid to him.

21st May 1839
Stolen on the night of 28th (April?) from a Brick Yard in Coronation Road: a white drake with a green beak. Property of Mr Wildgoose.

5th January 1840
At about 2.30pm PC 187 - Warren, found a pair of trousers and a waistcoat in Regent Street which he took to Bedminster Police Station and on enquiry the same were found to belong to a prisoner named Bailey, who had been found drunk in Coronation Road by PC 191 - Lewis, some time previously.

P C Ernest Stapleford joined the police force following service in the First World War. He was married in 1915 at East Street Baptist Chapel. He lived with his wife at 75 Stackpool Road.

SOUTHVILLE VOICES

Talk With Bert Brimble

I was born in 1894 in the country, near Timsbury. When my wife's father moved to the St Luke's area of Totterdown in the 1920s to establish a dairy, my family and I also moved to Bristol. I had been a miner for most of my life, so the dairy business seemed a wonderful change and indeed it was.

In 1931 I established my own small dairy at 22 Southville Place. Every morning I brought the milk down from St Luke's Road and sold it in Southville. I used a motor cycle and side car and had a big pail and churn as well as government measures and ladles for one pint and half pints. Milk cost 4d a pint and most people bought half pints. They would come out to get it with mugs, teapots, jamjars, any kind of container. Bottles did not come out until around 1938 as I recall. A man came around selling skimmed milk for one penny a pint. People said they bought it for their pets, but I think some poor folks used it themselves. Even though a lot of the people in the area were employed by Wills, the average wage was £2.10s then. Generally though Southville was 'upper crust'. There were many big houses on Coronation, Alpha, Acramans and Southville Roads.

Councillor Sampson had the big house, now the Vicarage, on Southville Road and Henry Jones, who had the flour mill on Dean Crescent, owned Mona Lodge, now the Chapel of Rest. Mrs. Friar later lived at Mona Lodge. Her father Mr. Clifford, lived on Coronation Road at No 51, I believe. Dr Lucas lived at No 48 Coronation Road. Dallens, the Sailmakers and Williams the Haulage Contractors lived nearby. The Ford Potato firm was on the corner of Acramans and Southville Road.

Fred Baker was landlord of the Southville Inn and it was very well kept. The pub opposite the park (Dame Emily's), The Clarence, was very popular. It had a white wooden step which was scrubbed and scrubbed and was always immaculate. Women didn't go to public houses very often then and my mother-in-law got very angry at my wife for going once.

Our houses in Southville Place were nice and we had church people and a police inspector as neighbours. But we didn't have bathrooms or hot water, just an outside lavatory. In fact our house was one of three on one waterpipe, so that when one family was using water, the others had none or just a trickle. Like other neighbourhoods we had different sorts of people. A musician who lived on the corner kept everyone awake by playing all night. One lady, Mrs. Williams I think, was always riding up and down Lucky Lane in a horse and gig, practising, I suppose. Johnson, the tailor, who lived nearby, kept sneezing because he always had snuff in his pockets, something to do with the dust of his trade.

Men in turbans came around selling things. I don't think they were from India. Tinkers pushed trolleys, repairing and sharpening knives. The rag and bone man always came before the ash men arrived and used horse and carts. There were two shops on the corner of Florence Place and they sold just about everything. Bread was 4d a loaf, one cwt of coal was 2/- and five Woodbines cost 2d. Groceries were ordered and brought around by a delivery boy. Horse and carts came by with fresh meat and vegetables. There were cottages all they way down the hill opposite Wills. I don't know if they were bombed later or pulled down.

It was a big event when a boat came down The Cut. Not many came then so that everyone would run out to see it. We had gas lighting until 1939 but then a lot of things changed. Once the whole area smelled of orange blossom and lilac. But it had been a good life for me in Southville.

Talk with Ernest Bray

Memories of Southville in the 1920s and 1930s.

The Bray family took over the running of the grocer's shop at 86 Stackpool Road in 1928. This shop was built as a house and General Store in the 1890s. The owner then was James Wakefield. Donald and Gilbert Bray ran the shop until 1935, when Donald took over a grocer's shop on the corner of Upton/Gathorne Road. Ernest continued to run the shop in Stackpool Road with his brother Gilbert until the War. It finally closed down in 1973.

During the time the Bray family ran the shop, it supplied goods to the school for use in the kitchens at Beauley Road and to many staff of the schools. Elementary and Senior School plus the Junior School teachers used to leave their baskets with orders to be made up during the day. Orders were also delivered to customers in the area.

Other grocer shops in Southville were Butts Stores, who had five shops locally, one at the bottom of Stackpool Road/Dean Lane, one at the bottom of Merrywood Road which later became Pitts Bakery, another on North Street, one in Totterdown and a warehouse in Merrywood road. The local Dairy was Barnets at the top of Merrywood Road. Later, in the 1930s, they opened a little shop selling milk, butter, ice-cream etc, but sold out to Unigate after the War.

Opposite the shop at 86 Stackpool Road, was a very large house which was the Doctor's house for the surgery at North Street. Various doctors who lived there were Dr Blacker, Dr Murray and Dr Sampson; they also had occasional surgeries there. Next to the Doctor's house towards Greville Street, was a showcase for a plumbing firm called Hassel. Other people living at the top end of Stackpool Road included the Quick family, three sons, all Bristol Rugby players, and a daughter. They were next door neighbours of the Miles family. Miles & Son were the large drapers near the London Inn, Cannon Street' until the 1970s.

The Southville Hotel (now The Imp) was run by a Mr Baker in the 1930s. His daughter Eileen was Secretary at Merrywood School, and later went to Knowle, when the school moved into thier new premises. The Clarence in Dean Lane was a very up-market pub in the 1930s. Avon Packet on Coronation Road had Paddy O'Brien as the Landlord. The Off-License on the corner of Greenway Bush Lane was run by Ted Fudge in the 1920s. Next door was Verrechias Ice-Cream Parlour, complete with glass-topped tables and cane chairs, the first, I believe, of Verrechias shops.

My uncle, Mr Alfred Bray (my uncle) built most of Hamilton Road and lived there (in a house which is just slightly larger than all the rest) for some while, then moved to 110 Coronation Road. Later he became a partner with Bray & Slaughter, and built several houses in Osborne Road (two semi detached and one detached) in 1935.

Appendix
SOUTHVILLE STREETS AND PLACES
Dates of construction or completion.

1821	Trafalgar Place	(Coronation Road)	1872	Lombard Street	
			1873	Essex Street	
1822	Coronation Road		1874	Catherine Mead Street	
			1875	Greenway Road	
1825	Charlotte Street			Sidney Street	
			1879	North Place	
1828	Alpha Cottages	(Coronation Road)		Stackpool Road	
	Wellington Terrace	..	1880	Pembroke Road	
	Richmond Place	..	1882	Greville Street	
	King Street	..	1883	Greville Road	
	Queen Street		1883/84	Osborne Road	
			1885	Edgware Road	
1829	Greenway Place	(Dean Lane)		Islington Road	
1830	Carlton Place	(North Street)		Allington Road	
1831	Farley's Square		1886	Camden Road	
1839	Dean Street		1887	Argyle Street	
1844	Mount Pleasant	(Coronation Road)	1888	Milford Street	
	Coronation Buildings	..		Summer Street	
				Hill Street	
				Upper Perry Hill	
1845	Greenway Bush Lane				
	Ashton Terrace	(Coronation Road)	1890	Park Road	
1847	Southville Road			Warden Road	
	Alpha Road			Howard Road	
1848	Mount Pleasant Terrace			Dalston Road	
1850	Ashton Place				
1853	Russell Terrace		1893	Morley Road	
	Nelson Terrace	(Coronation Road)	1894	Kingston Road	
1858	Clarence Place			Merrywood Lane	
	Southville Place			(re-named Merrywood Road)	
	Florence Place			Vicarage Road	
1861	Laura Villas	(Alpha Road)	1897	Beauley Road	
1870	Acramans Road			Upper part of Stackpool Road	
	Coronation Villas		1898	Exmoor Street	
	Greenbank Road			Leighton Road	
	Greenbank Villas			Gathorne Road	
	Greenbank Terrace		1899-1900		
	Bull Lane			Raleigh Road	
	(re-named Merrywood Lane)		1900	Hamilton Road	
	New Charlotte Street			Birch Road	
	Southville Road			Upton Road	
	Union road			Fairfield Road	
	Regent Road		1902	Exeter Road	
1871	Ashton Road			Lime Road	
	Herbert Street		1919	Lydstep Terrace	
	King William Street				

SOURCES AND ACKNOWLEDGEMENTS

Arrowsmith; Mr Anton Bantock; Bedminster Library (Bristol City Council); Bedminster Quarter Sessions Records; Board of Governors, Southville Primary School(1987); Bristol Record Office; Census Returns: 1801,1841,1851; Bristol Past and Present, published by Nichols and Taylor(1860); Mr P Cleeve; The Clifton Chronicles; Mrs. Elsie Everitt; Felix Farley's Journals; H C W Harris: The Origin of District and Street Names in Bristol; Kelly's Directory; Latimer: Annals of the 18th Century; Matthews Directory; Ogilby: Road Map (1698); St.Paul's Graveyard Records; Zion Church Records.

Photographs are from C.L.A.S.S. members archive with the exception of the following: Front cover, photograph reproduced by kind permission of Reece Winstone Archive and Publishing; Page 3, photograph by kind permission of 'Memories', Old Photographic Prints, Corn Exchange, Bristol; Pages 10 and 11, photographs reproduced by kind permission of Imperial Tobacco Limited; Page 27, photograph by Roy Gallop.

Line drawings: Back cover and title page by S J Loxton, reproduced by kind permission of Bristol City Council Central Library; Page 30, Etching, artist unidentified, from Bristol Past and Present, Nichols and Taylor; Page 38, etching taken from W H Pyne's Rustic Vignettes for Artists and Craftsmen, published by Dover Publications Inc., 1977.
Maps: Pages 5 and 26, by Roy Gallop; Page, 33, by Glyn Williams.
Additional typing sevices by Leighanne Gough.
The publishers acknowledge not only the help and support given by Mrs. Joy Gardner of Southville, but her tenacity in keeping the project alive in the expectation of publication.

In many cases the photographs reproduced in this book are by unidentified photographers or cannot be located. If the publishers have unintentionally infringed copyright we apologise and if informed we will remedy in any subsequent edition.

Other titles available from good booksellers or by post from Fiducia Press, 10 Fairfield Road, Bristol BS3 1LG (telephone 0117 9 852795)

Fussells Ironworks, Mells	£5.00
The Glastonbury Canal	£5.00
The Parrett Navigation	£4.00
The Coaching Era	£6.50
The Gentle Giants (Bristol Shire Horses)	£3.00
Recollections of Chew Magna (1930-40)	£5.00
Recollections of Jazz in Bristol	£10.00
Dave Collett Blues	£3.00
Views of Labour and Gold	£10.00
Smaller Towns of Somerset	£4.95
The Severn Tunnel	£19.95

Poetry:
Manly Monodes

26 alliterative poems	£3.00
Tracts from the Tracks	
The Ridgeway Poems	£5.00
Selected Poems	
A Personal Journey	£3.00

Past Somerset Times
Illustrated Studies of the County's Rich History
Volume 1
£5.00

All orders post free. Full list of titles on request.